uitment and Sampling:
Qualitative Research with
Older People

Edited by Caroline Holland

NUMBER 5 IN

THE REPRESENTATION OF OLDER PEOPLE IN AGEING RESEARCH SERIES

The Open
University

First published in 2005
by the Centre for Policy on Ageing
25-31 Ironmonger Row
London EC1V 3QP
Tel: +44 (0)20 7553 6500
Fax: +44 (0)20 7553 6501
Email: cpa@cpa.org.uk
Website: www.cpa.org.uk

Registered charity no 207163

British Library Cataloguing in Publication Data
A catalogue record for this book is available from the British Library

ISBN 1 901097 95 1

The Representation of Older People in Ageing Research Series is based on
seminars organised by the Centre for Ageing and Biographical Studies, Faculty of
Health and Social Care, the Open University, and the Centre for Policy on
Ageing. The papers in this volume have been revised and new material added
since the seminar took place.

Titles in the series:

Biographical Interviews: the link between research and practice, edited by Joanna
Bornat (No 1)

*Involving Older People in Research: 'an amateur doing the work of a
professional?',* edited by Sheila Peace (No 2)

Writing Old Age, edited by Julia Johnson (No 3)

Everyday Living in Later Life, edited by Bill Bytheway (No 4)

Making Observations, edited by Sheila Peace (No 6)

Printed in the United Kingdom by Henry Ling Limited,
at the Dorset Press, Dorchester DT1 1HD

CONTENTS

1

SOME ISSUES IN RECRUITING AND SAMPLING FROM THE OLDER POPULATION

CAROLINE HOLLAND

Recruitment and sampling are important in social gerontology because they directly affect research findings. As Thomas Scharf comments in chapter 3, there is also an increasing imperative in ageing research to include older people as more than sampled subjects. Positioning this changed perspective within a wider development in the social sciences, the Director of the ESRC's 'Growing Older' Programme has stated: 'This change is critical for a variety of reasons and, especially, because it sensitises science to the perspectives of older people and attempts to treat them as partners in the research process' (Walker 2002). The research projects described in this collection have engaged with older people in different ways, with consequent effects on the relationship between 'researcher' and 'researched', and between both of them and the data (see Peace 1999).

But who exactly are we sampling? How are we recruiting? We know that the population of older people in the UK is increasingly large and diverse and, as the proportion of older people increases relative to younger people, of increasing prominence. Arguably, for most of its history, gerontology in the UK has tended to emphasise biological/problematic ageing, and to reflect social policy and welfare agendas (Phillipson and Biggs 1999). These are agendas that continue to be highly significant in themselves and they also have an impact on the funding available for research. But interest in the lives of older people now goes well beyond this traditional focus and researchers in other fields as well as in gerontology are increasingly interested in ageing. The EPSRC's EQUAL[1] programme on extending quality of life in old age, for example, included projects involving engineers, designers, technologists, computer scientists, architects, biologists and many others. All of these researchers, many of them 'new to ageing', are now sampling the older

---

1 The EQUAL Programme ran from to 1997 to 2004, with three waves of projects.

population and recruiting older people to the qualitative elements of various studies.

The papers collected together in this volume describe five quite different studies of ageing and intergenerational relationships. The methodologies and sample sizes involved range from Montague's micro-level study of relationships between a small group of friends, to the multi-method approach of Scharf et al., incorporating interviews with people identified from a larger survey. Each of the studies has taken a different approach to recruiting older people and involving them in the research process and, from them, we can see the emergence of some common themes that have also been reflected in other recent research. These include: 'vulnerability' and ethics; the role of the gatekeeper; under- and over-researched groups; sensitive topics and the role of language; and older people as research partners. In considering these themes I draw here also on participative research currently being undertaken by members of CABS, and on some of the projects from the Growing Older Programme (see Newsletters 4 and 5 in particular),[2] where most of the 24 'GO' projects included some qualitative research.

'VULNERABILITY' AND THE ETHICS OF RECRUITMENT

Before fieldwork is started, research usually requires the approval of one or more ethics committees. Social scientists have long worked to professional standards such as those of the Social Research Association or the British Psychological Society, and taken projects for approval to ethics committees. Many projects must now be considered by LREC or MREC[3] committees, and researchers also need to consider the Department of Health Research Governance Framework and Criminal Records Bureau clearances for people working with 'vulnerable' participants.

Thomas Scharf (chapter 3) discusses in detail the process he encountered in seeking ethical approval from LRECs for his project. He acknowledges that the process can help to refine the research design as well as allowing protection for participants, researchers and research

---

2 The Growing Older Programme (GO) ran from 1999 to 2004 and involved 24 projects under the Directorship of Professor Alan Walker. All the GO Project Findings and the Newsletters I have referenced here were made available at - http://www.shef.ac.uk/uni/projects/gop

3 Local Research Ethics Committees relate to research within single strategic authorities and Multiple Research Ethics Committees to research within more than one strategic authority.

funders; yet he found that the nature of qualitative social research was still poorly understood by some ethics committees. In Scharf's case, the research team opted to re-think their recruitment method so that they could be sure to complete their fieldwork within the time frame of the project and remain consistent to the ethical demands of this kind of research. But this experience is a cautionary tale about the tensions between gaining ethical approval, the recruitment of research participants, and the design and time-tabling of projects.

One of the projects currently being undertaken by CABS members, in partnership with Help the Aged, is the 'RoAD' project – Research on Age Discrimination. This is a two-year project funded by the Community Fund/Big Red Lottery and led by Bill Bytheway. Large numbers of older people are being recruited as panellists, correspondents, and focus group members, and the project has so far trained around a dozen older people as researchers to interview older people who are keeping diaries about their everyday experiences of age discrimination. The fieldworkers have been carefully recruited to carry out sensitive interviews with people who may be particularly vulnerable. The fieldworkers have been cleared by the Criminal Records Bureau and procedures have been put in place to refer interviewees to support systems where necessary. In training and supporting the fieldworkers and putting these risk reduction procedures in place, the research team have tried to anticipate and circumvent any problems that might result from taking part in the research – in essence, this is what an ethical approach demands. But putting all this in place has taken a lot of time and money, and as the ways of involving older people in research become more complex, it is clear that this aspect of research will need to be adequately resourced.

So, having secured the necessary funding and/or researcher time, and having sought and gained ethical approval for the planned methodology, the next stage is to find the research participants – and as we see from the papers collected here, there are very many ways of doing this. In one of the Growing Older projects, 'Environment and Identity in Later Life; a cross-setting study', Sheila Peace, Leonie Kellaher and I wanted a sample of people who were living in different types of housing in different kinds of urban/rural locations. We also wanted people to take part in the project at three different levels – focus groups; one-to-one interviews; and on video – requiring different levels of self-disclosure. Our recruitment methods for the interviews included: leafleting clubs and individual houses in the target areas; personal contacts with gatekeepers in organisations specifically for older people or likely to include older people; recruitment from earlier focus groups; snowballing; and personal contacts. We found participants for the video from among those who had been interviewed. But it was in the first stage of the research, when we were arranging focus groups in various places, that we occasionally encountered resistance from gatekeepers who thought that their club members or residents would not be interested in our research. The gatekeeper role – both in blocking and in facilitating contact between researchers and potential participants – is one that recurs in descriptions by researchers of their experience in recruiting research participants.

GATEKEEPERS

Several other projects in the Growing Older programme reported difficulties with gatekeepers in organisations. Hughes et al. (2002) for example experienced resistance from minority ethnic/cultural based organisations. Withnall (2002) found that, when negotiating access to groups of older learners to invite them to take part in focus groups, it was younger gatekeepers who were the most likely to decide against inviting them. Likewise when Davidson et al. (2002) conducted research into the social lives and health lifestyles of older men, they encountered differences in the behaviour of gatekeepers in different organisations: while managers of statutory and voluntary clubs for older people were amenable to the research, managers of private sport and leisure clubs not specifically for older people were more guarded. This probably reflects different attitudes to 'members' in different kinds of organisations as much as attitudes to research, but Davidson makes the good point that gatekeepers do need to be convinced themselves about the relevance of the proposed research before the researcher can hope to convince potential participants. In addition, as Warren et al. (2002, p. 4) comment regarding their experience: 'Gatekeepers to groups were uniformly over-worked and under-funded, and commitment to the project constituted an additional drain on their time and resources.'

In their study of the impact of family change, Peace et al. (chapter 5) sought a purposive sample of people to interview, including different generations of families that had been affected by breakdown and reconstitution. Peace describes how the first year of the study became dominated by the attempt to achieve this sample through area screening. The researchers found that while individuals were willing to talk about their own experiences, they were generally unwilling to facilitate access to younger and older generations within their own family. In this case, and also in Jane Montague's doctoral study described in chapter 2, the gatekeepers were key individuals rather than representatives of organisations.

In her study, it is clear that the research method Montague decided to use was largely dictated by the kind of data that she was aiming to collect – familiar talk about relationships between people who knew each other. Coupled with her desire to be an 'insider' in the conversations rather than an 'outsider', this meant that her recruitment method involved the tactic, fairly unusual in the social sciences, of starting with her own family members and moving out from them to recruit their friends in conversational dyads. The effect of this recruitment method was to produce the kind of talk – familiar, relaxed, sometimes assuming prior knowledge – that would enable her to analyse at a very fine level how women construct and continue their close relationships in such conversations. Montague both selected people very specifically for the project, and allowed recruits to suggest others to join them (and indeed 'de-select' people on the basis of unsuitability). While such an approach would be entirely unsuitable for many studies, it suited Montague's research needs well and had the additional merit of avoiding the discomfort that some respondents felt in Peace's description of trying to recruit family groups.

Montague's sample, while small and very specific, was not difficult for her to identify or access. In other cases, the required sample is more elusive – for example because the population in question is over-researched, 'invisible', or difficult to reach.

SAMPLING AND RECRUITING FROM MINORITY GROUPS

Certain groups have been described as particularly 'invisible' in the UK – including Chinese older people (Jones 1998); and Jewish older people (Valins 2002). While Jewish communities in the UK have a much older age profile than the general population, older Jews may be difficult to sample because of problems of definition and recording (Valins 2002). Yet some researchers have found that particular Black Caribbean and other accessible groups have been over-researched: 'older people often felt they had been "researched to death" over the past 15 years' (Butt and O'Neil 2004). This applies for example to groups accessed through community organisations in places where specific minority communities have a visible presence (Afshar et al. 2002; Warren et al. 2002). There have also been suggestions of 'mining' data from disadvantaged groups, where researchers are seen to have swooped in, gathered their data, and left nothing of clear benefit to the researched (Sin 2004). While this takes us back to the point about keeping people informed and convinced about the significance of the research, it also suggests that sampling people from minority cultural groups can present something of a challenge. Blakemore and Boneham (2004) suggested that there is widespread avoidance of census enumeration in the Black-Caribbean community and, while most Black-Caribbean and Asian older people are registered with GPs, not every research project would be able to access them in this way. It is perhaps not surprising then that clubs are often the starting point for researchers unfamiliar with particular communities. Yet as with other clubs and organisations, the people who have not joined them, including those too poor or unwell to take part, are excluded from samples reached this way. Furthermore Sin (2004) cites a study by McLeod et al. (2001) which found that less than 30 per cent of interviewees from a BME background were able to name a specifically BME voluntary or community organisation: 'The implication is that those who are in touch with such organisations are unrepresentative of the wider population' (p. 266).

So how else might we recruit samples of older participants from minority ethnic or cultural groups? We see in chapter 3 that Scharf's use of MONICA to identify older people in the community worked well enough for English-speaking white people and Black-Caribbean people, but not for other ethnic groups. There have been some attempts to identify, for example, people of Asian origin, by name. Atkin et al. (1989) found that only 1 per cent of people with non-Asian names in a sample of people in central Birmingham were of Asian origin, while 6 per cent of people with Asian names were non-Asian by origin or self-identification. However this method, unlike MONICA, does not identify older people within these communities, and in any case the definition of 'older' here may need to be more flexible (Sin 2004).

With both numbers and proportions of older people from BME groups set to rise for the foreseeable future, it is important that their needs and opinions feature in research alongside those of the diverse groups within the majority ethnic population – and research funders often require this perspective. In practice, however, it can be difficult in small-scale studies to move beyond a tokenistic representation and we perhaps need to be clear about what our sampling is designed to achieve and whether our recruitment processes help to achieve it.

As Nazroo and Grewal (2002) point out, practical constraints often mean that recruitment from minority ethnic groups is carried out by white recruiters in the English language – an alternative is to attempt ethnic matching, for example between an interviewer and a respondent. This approach was attempted by some of the Growing Older projects with some success in terms of recruitment and the quality of data (Nazroo and Grewal; Butt et al.) but there was discussion about this issue within the Programme and researchers acknowledged some of the problems. How close a match in ethnic identity? Given the multi-faceted nature of peoples' identities, should we prioritise ethnicity over gender and class? Is language the issue rather than ethnicity? How does translation affect direct researcher-participant communication?

Another even larger group of older people who are seen to have been under-represented in research are older men. Fennell and Davidson (2003, p. 316) comment: 'It is somewhat ironic that the discipline of gerontology derives its roots from the Greek, geron-otos meaning "old man" … and yet until comparatively recently, older men largely have been neglected in social research on ageing.' Old age, it is claimed, has been largely feminised, partly because of the comparative size and visibility of the population of older women and partly because the organisation of social facilities has often been geared toward the needs of older widowed women. Older men often feel outnumbered and edged out in community activities, and this can also apply to sheltered housing (Fennell and Davidson 2003).

In one of two Growing Older projects that specifically looked at bereavement, Bennett et al. (2002) focused on the lifestyle of people who had been widowed in later life. In their search for participants, the researchers found widowed women easy to access via groups and snowballing. Men on the other hand had to be approached more indirectly (for example via a related study) and as individuals, rather than from within groups. This project also raised the issue of what researchers may or may not be prepared to do to find their sample: 'We were not able to recruit from pubs, bookmakers' shops, or cafes attended by men because the women on the team felt inhibited' (Hughes et al. 2002). This consideration might also apply to researchers entering other 'foreign territories' although it is not an issue that is much discussed.

SENSITIVE TOPICS

Rebecca Jones (chapter 4) raises the issue of the language that we use to describe our research and to recruit people to participate in it. Jones starts from the premise that the knowledge we generate in research depends on the cultural context in which it is conducted. She makes it clear that how you introduce and explain what your research is about has a major effect on the outcomes. This is especially important when, as in her case, the subject of the research can be seen as a sensitive one; or indeed when the targeted group of participants is seen as especially vulnerable. In spite of thinking carefully about this from the outset and trying to avoid introducing the topic in loaded terms, Jones did find herself 'somewhat reluctantly, treating the topic as both sensitive and delicate'. This in turn had an effect on the kind of people who took part in the research and the kind of data that was generated by it.

In the stepfamilies project, described by Peace et al. in chapter 5, the researchers were also aware of the importance of language as they attempted to recruit people in a way that would enable them to obtain the kind of information they wanted. They avoided the use of the word 'step' as a defining term in family relationships, to try to reach people who were not necessarily defining themselves in those terms. Even so, talking about family breakdown and reconstitution, at least between family members, proved to be more sensitive than they had anticipated.

The other GO project that focused on bereavement was led by Peter Coleman, in this case looking at the role of spiritual beliefs on adjustment to bereavement. From this work, Coleman has suggested that research with this degree of sensitivity can bear certain parallels to counselling. As in counselling, the research relationship needs to have a 'beginning', 'middle' and 'end'. He reminds us that recruitment might not be a 'one-off' event because there is a continuing need to keep people on-board and informed; and there must be scope in the research design for people to withdraw.

INVOLVING OLDER PEOPLE AS RESEARCH PARTNERS

But first people must be recruited to take part, and it is at this stage that the purpose of the project and the nature of involvement must be explained. Potential recruits will typically want to know: What is the research about? Who are you, and why do you want to study this? What do you want from me? What will I get out of it? What good will it be?

Social gerontologists have been used to the participation of older people based on their altruistic desire to 'help others in the future', 'improve things', 'help science', or even 'help you with your studies'. The expectation of altruistic involvement is wearing a bit thin though for some older people today – including people in the groups that feel themselves to be over-researched; people who are very busy; people who are very private – and those just not feeling particularly altruistic at the time. As we increasingly involve older people in research in more demanding ways, some questions arise: What is reasonable to ask of volunteers? Should people be paid for their time/involvement? What are the implications of more participative research methods?

The most commonly used qualitative research methods involve group discussions and interviews with individuals, perhaps alongside other methods such as surveys and measures. These have their own demands and occasionally participants drop out for whatever reason; but some of the more innovative methods of involvement can place higher demands upon participants. In one of the Growing Older projects, Alexandra Withnall wanted to look at the role of learning in the post-work period of life. As part of the data collection, people were recruited to keep diaries over a three-month period. Withnall found that this task proved to be too onerous for many of the participants and commented that the method should perhaps be adapted in future research to allow the tape recording of diaries, or keeping them over shorter time periods. Bytheway and Johnson (2003) in an earlier book in this series, have described their use of diaries over just two weeks in a study of older people's management of long-term medication. Diaries are being used again in the RoAD project with the option for people to record or phone-in their diary entries.

On the other hand, Andrew Clark refers in chapter 6 to the commitment of a small number of older participants who have carried out observations outdoors right through the winter months. This is a group of people that is largely self-selected: many more we presume thought about it and decided not to get involved. But in most cases there is an element of self-selection in those who agree to take part in research. This is not usually a problem as long as it is acknowledged and attention given to its possible impact upon the extent to which generalised conclusions can be drawn. Another important point about Clark's observers is that they are paid for their involvement, on the understanding that their role as co-researchers goes beyond what is usually demanded of research participants.

In research generally and certainly within the Growing Older programme, there have been different views about whether, and how much, research participants should be recompensed for their involvement. Some of the GO researchers were strongly of the view that paying participants could potentially distort research findings; make it difficult for non-paying projects to recruit people; and increase the costs of research or make some projects unaffordable. Some projects, in addition to the standard practice of providing participants with 'findings'/summaries of the research, also gave them honoraria including gift vouchers, special meals, and 'GO' pottery mugs. Paying cash for participants' time is more controversial. It is understood in medical ethics that participants in clinical trials should not be induced to take part by the offer of payment, but in social research the principles of good practice tend to allow the possibility of payments provided that participation is voluntary, informed, and does not 'involve unwarranted material gain or loss for any participant'[4] (The Respect Code of Practice). It has been argued that *not* paying the expenses of participants potentially excludes those who put a greater value on their own time, energy and views (as general practitioners and other professionals tend to), and may 'leave residues' about how the researcher has valued the participants' time (Thompson 1996). As research increasingly engages older people more fully as research partners (for example Leamy and Clough 2001; Warren 2002; the RoAD project described above, and Social Interactions project described in chapter 6), researchers need to get to grips with this issue.

CONCLUSION

Given the diversity of older people, sampling for research and recruiting for participation in research are never going to be simple matters. Older people have multiple roles and identities; different circumstances, health, wealth, social class, ethnicity, and education; varied living conditions and arrangements. We should expect to use different strategies to identify and recruit older research partners according to their life styles. Researchers cannot assume that all older people are willing to be passive sources of data, nor that they all want to be deeply involved. We need to be clear about the nature of the commitment we are asking from them, and what we are offering as recompense either as payment, information, or real

---

4 The European Commission's Respect Code of Practice, section 3; see http://www.respectproject.org/code/

practical outcomes. Having decided upon a particular methodology, this should be tested and the implications for research outcomes carefully considered.

New ways of working with older people as more involved partners require more detailed planning, higher costs, and more management, and these need to be taken into account from the outset. However this can be more problematic where researchers and older people want to work together on the research design and bidding for funding before they are able to secure either ethical approval or the costs of such early involvement. In addition, where older people are to be recruited as co-researchers, interviewers, etc., having a direct practical input for which they are paid, there are issues about their contractual status, training, and management that also have to be resolved.

Taking seriously the voices of older people from minority ethnic and cultural groups requires work, including 'inputs of time and energy to build trust and demonstrate commitment' (Warren 2002). Language, ever important in the exchange of complex ideas between researchers and respondents, takes on a particular significance here. Some researchers have found that shared origins and language can help in the discussion of sensitive topics (Butt et al. 2002); and even when English is used, it helps to understand the cultural context of particular terms or phrases. Of course this also apples more generally, as Rebecca Jones' chapter shows.

The main message seems to be that in being reflexive about the processes of qualitative research and the positioning of 'researcher' and 'researched', the sampling and recruitment stage should not be omitted. It would be good to think that future research reports would, like the papers here, be more open about how sampling and recruitment were approached and how they affected the research outcomes.

REFERENCES

Afshar, H., Franks, M., Maynard, M. and Wray, S. (2002) Issues of ethnicity in researching older women. *ESRC Growing Older Programme Newsletter* 4, pp. 8–9.

Atkin, K., Evers, H., Badger, F. and Cameron, E. (1989) *The Community Care Project: Survey of Older Asians and Non-Asians: Aims and Methods*. Working Paper 21, Health Services' Research Centre, University of Birmingham. Cited in Sin (2004) op. cit.

Bennett, K., Smith, P. and Hughes, G. (2002) Older widow(er)s: bereavement and gender effects on lifestyle and participation. *GO Findings* 6, September.

Blakemore, K. and Boneham, M. (1994) *Age, Race and Ethnicity: A Comparative Approach*. Buckingham: Open University Press.

Butt, J. and O'Neil, A. (2004) *Black and Minority Ethnic Older People's Views on Research Findings*. May 2004, Findings 564. York: Joseph Rowntree Foundation.

Butt, J., Moriarty, J., Brockmann, M. and Sin, C. H. (2002) Interviewing black and minority ethnic older people. *ESRC Growing Older Programme Newsletter* 4, pp. 7–8.

Bytheway, B. and Johnson, J. (2003) Every day's the same? A study of the management of long-term medication, in B. Bytheway (ed) *Everyday Living in Later Life*. The Representation of Older People in Ageing Research Series, No 4. London: Centre for Policy on Ageing.

Davidson, K., Daly, T. and Arber, S. (2003) Older men, social integration, and organisational activities. *Social Policy and Society* 2(2): 81–89.

Fennell, G. and Davidson, K. (2003) "The Invisible Man?" Older men in modern society. *Ageing International* 28(4): 315–325.

Hughes, G., Bennett, K. and Smith, P. (2002) Older widow(er)s: bereavement and gender effects on lifestyle and participation – recruitment and retention. *ESRC Growing Older Programme Newsletter* 5, p. 3.

Jones, A. (1998) The invisible minority: the housing needs of Chinese older people in England. School of Public Policy Occasional Paper, No 16. University of Birmingham.

Leamy, M. and Clough, R. (2001) Older people as researchers: their role in a research project. *Education and Ageing* 16(3).

McLeod, M., Owen, D. and Khamis, C. (2001) *Black and Minority Ethnic Voluntary and Community Organisations: Their Role and Future Development in England and Wales*. London: Policy Studies Institute for the Joseph Rowntree Foundation.

Nazroo, J. and Grewal, I. (2002) Qualitative methods for investigating ethnic inequalities: lessons from a study of quality of life among older people. *ESRC Growing Older Programme Newsletter* 4, pp. 2–3.

Peace, S. (1999) *Involving Older People in Research: 'An Amateur Doing the Work of a Professional?'* The Representation of Older People in Ageing Research Series, No 2. London: Centre for Policy on Ageing.

Phillipson, C. and Biggs, S. (1999) Population ageing: critical gerontology and the sociological tradition. *Education and Ageing* 14(2): 159–170.

Sin, Chih Hoong (2004) Sampling minority ethnic older people in Britain. *Ageing and Society* 24(2): 257–277.

Thompson, S. (1996) Paying respondents and informants. *Social Research Update,* No 14. Department of Sociology, University of Surrey.

Valins, O. (2002) *Facing the Future: The Provision of Long-term Care Facilities for Older Jewish People in the United Kingdom.* London: Institute for Jewish Policy Research.

Walker, A. (2002) Introduction to *ESRC Growing Older Programme Newsletter* 5, p. 1.

Warren, L., Cook, J. and Maltby, T. (2002) Working with older women from communities in Sheffield: methods issues. *ESRC Growing Older Programme Newsletter* 4, pp. 3–5.

Withnall, A. (2002) Involving older people in research on lifelong learning: lessons for the future. *ESRC Growing Older Programme Newsletter* 5, pp. 4–5.

2

RESEARCHING RELATIONSHIPS IN TALK AMONGST WOMEN WHO ARE PERSONALLY CONNECTED

JANE MONTAGUE

In this chapter I discuss some of the issues I encountered in recruiting research participants for a small-scale, detailed study of conversation about personal relationships. In earlier work I had perceived that, in general, social psychology tended to concentrate on investigating particular, single, aspects of relationships, including such characteristics as aggression, attraction and so on; rather than relationships in their totality (Miell and Dallos 1996). My initial focus on long-term partnerships developed in opposition to this fragmentation and in the research discussed here, I wanted to draw attention to the importance of the developmental aspects of relationships as a whole and over time, instead of simply looking at one specific part of, or time in, a relationship. In addition to these concerns, it was also notable that psychological research exploring the lives of older people tended to concentrate on the cognitive deterioration and decline that takes place in older age groups. In contrast my research examines some of the more positive aspects of older people's lives particularly around the continuity of their personal relationships. The method I used to recruit participants in this research was crucial to the kind of data that would be generated.

DEVELOPING THE RESEARCH: SOME PRIMARY ISSUES

My interest in the field of personal relationships crystallised during my undergraduate degree in psychology and led to my final-year dissertation – a discursive examination of the development and changes in the long-term relationships of five older women with their marital partners (Montague and Stokoe 1998). In that piece of research I used a semi-structured format in two ways. I first audio-recorded a conversation individually with each of the participants, and then I videotaped a group discussion between all five, prompted by the same set of questions. The breadth of topics discussed and information given differed in each stage: intimate in the one-to-one conversations, but much more general in the group discussion.

Continuing this general approach into my doctoral research study, at an early stage in the process I recorded a conversation with Ada, an older friend of mine. In this I wanted to investigate particular issues to do with being married in the years before, during and after the Second World War. However, contrary to my expectations, Ada's account of her first year of marriage hardly featured the relationship that I had considered would be the most significant. Normative expectations around early married life – that talk about being newly married would focus on managing the new relationship – had been echoed in my previous research, and I expected the questions I asked Ada to generate talk about the problems and issues linked to this. Instead, the conversation revolved around Ada's relationship with her sister and brother-in-law with whom she shared a house, whilst her new husband was employed at the other end of the country. Her husband actually featured little in the conversation.

By trying to concentrate on that one relationship, whilst ignoring the context in which it was embedded, I echoed social psychology's absorption with individual aspects of relationships at the expense of looking at the whole picture. Attempting to limit conversation to one relationship is impossible because all relationships are located in a network of many and inevitably talk about one will introduce talk about others that link with it (Ickes and Duck 2000).

Another issue – and the one that played a large part in determining my final group of participants – related to my chosen methodology. Social scientists tend to investigate relationships by administering either surveys or questionnaires (Ickes 2000), both of which use a format agreed upon by the researcher/s beforehand. The research may be quantitative and include the formulation of a hypothesis, or it may be qualitative with one or more research questions. In either case questions are standardised and rigorously focused around the researcher(s) agenda. This leads conventionally to a separation of the researcher from the researched with much discussion centring on the dichotomy between those doing the studying and those being studied. More recently however the need for a greater awareness of the role that the researcher plays has been highlighted, both in the data generation process itself and also in the analysis of the ensuing data (Kanuha 2000).

In my dissertation study, using the same questions in both the individual and group conversations had generated different responses and showed that, even within a relatively stringent 'researcher directed' context, participants play an important part in determining what information is made relevant. The separation of the researcher from the researched was impossible. To take this into account I aimed in the second piece of research for a more balanced discussion, with my own role less as 'interviewer' and more as 'ordinary participant'. This move fitted my analytic frame of mixing the two ethnomethodological approaches of conversation analysis (CA) and membership categorisation analysis (MCA) (Watson 1997).

THE METHOD

In this research I used two stages of data generation. First I talked to each of the participants individually about relationships, using if necessary six or seven very general questions as conversational prompts. These interactions happened at times and places agreed between the participants and myself, but were much less 'directed' than if I had carried out an interview. They took the shape of what Burgess (1988) has termed a 'purposeful conversation'. So, although each conversation followed a similar pattern – we met at the home of the participant and I arrived with my set of conversational prompts – each one unfolded very differently depending upon the woman involved. Rather than taking the standardised shape of an interview, each of the conversations assumed its own pattern.

In the second stage, rather than simply building on the first stage with further individual interviews, the participants were invited to discuss their relationships in pairs using personal photographs as a topic to talk around. Personal objects – and particularly photographs – have been used successfully in various types of social scientific research. An existing body of work explicating this method of photo-elicitation (c.f. Plummer 2001; Prosser and Schwarz 1998; Radley and Taylor 2003) generally involves the researcher supplying visual stimuli and asking participants to talk about them. Personal photograph collections are biographically significant to many people (Rose 2003), and looking at them can be an important activity – for example to show off new members of the family, or as holiday mementoes or records of special occasions. Therefore, in my aim to access more intimate talk about relationships with my participants I invited them to talk about their own familiar photographs.

One advantage of this strategy was that they were able to include whoever they wanted in the conversations, and very rich discussions were prompted around diverse networks that included family members, friends, work colleagues and so on – the cast of the conversations seemed limitless. Many twists and turns relating to the photographs occurred and though talk sometimes seemed to veer 'off track' it generally returned to the topic of relationships. With my analytic focus on minute parts of conversational information I concentrated on explicating how a conversation is structured – how it actually happens (Sacks 1992). This type of research requires a different type of data than that gained by the traditional methods of investigation such as surveys and questionnaires.

During the planning of the research I realised that not only was it necessary for all of the women to be part of an existing relationship network, but that my own links to them were central to the study. My also being known to them was a necessity: my relationship with them enabled me to take part fully in the conversations as a 'familiar' person rather than just 'being there' as a researcher. The resulting series of conversations, though located in the context of research-focused interactions, had the mundane quality that yielded the type of very rich data I wanted. They replicated and represented the types of conversations that often take place in everyday life. In addition the network links between us became a further focus for analysis. The ways that people talk together are determined by the relationships between them: strangers will talk differently together than friends; work colleagues than lovers, and so on (Coupland, Coupland and Giles 1991). In this series of conversations we constructed relationships in the ways that we talked about them. At the same time, our relationships played a major part, through the fluidity of identity positions, in the ways that the conversations developed.

RECRUITMENT PROCESS: THE RELATIONSHIP NETWORK

As the recruitment of the participants and the nature of the subsequent conversations are linked closely together, I discuss here these links[1] and give examples to show how the relationships were made relevant and 'artfully' managed within the conversations.

Recruiting my first participant was extremely opportunistic in that I asked my mother, Marie, who had also been involved in my previous study, to take part and asked her to suggest other women connected to

1 I include myself here as a participant. To clarify my different identities in my data analysis i.e. as both researcher and participant I refer to myself as 'I' – the researcher; and 'Jane' – the participant.

her who she thought might also be interested.[2] Using this procedure throughout the recruitment, the final group consisted of women suggested by each other rather than being solely chosen by me – an aspect important to my overall aim of having an 'undirected' character to the research. This early conversation, along with some of those I recorded, proved useful in determining who was thought to be a 'good' participant for this project – not only in my own view but also in the opinion of the women themselves. It was particularly evident in the part played by Marie who, acting as a filter for my ideas, helped me form the initial list of possible participants. For instance, I proposed one particular woman who Marie discounted because 'she never talks'. This aspect was echoed later in the research during my conversation with Kate:

1. K   I don't know whether Julia would (.) next (.) across the road (.) now
2.   she's the loveliest person that you could possibly meet but she's so::o
3.   quiet and reserved

Both of these instances suggested that a 'good' participant was someone who would find it easy to talk in 'normal' circumstances – someone who was not 'quiet and reserved', and so would find no difficulty in talking in the contrived setting of a research conversation.

Based on my familiarity with previous research participants and my initial conversation with Marie, I next attempted to recruit Ethel and Kitty, who had both been involved in the earlier study and had said I should get in touch if I needed to talk to them again. However, neither of these attempts was successful. Ethel was apologetic but said she must refuse because her increasing hearing difficulties made conversation problematic for her. She was particularly conscious of having to ask for things to be repeated – a 'good' participant therefore had to not just be someone who would talk but who must also be able to hear and respond clearly. Kitty cited failing health of a different kind: she agreed at first to take part but subsequently changed her mind because of her increasingly frequent stays in hospital. This issue of inaccessibility was highlighted to me again later in relation to one of my participants who, though very willing to take part, was difficult to pin down to an available time.

---

2 Throughout the paper I refer to each of the women by their pseudonym rather than by their relationship to me or each other. However, these relationships are often made relevant by them in the conversations.

Similarly part of the conversation with Rebecca about a potential participant focussed on the difficulty of having time to participate:

```
1.  J      I've thought about Jane but she's always busy isn't she she's always
2.         scurrying about
3.  R      yes (.) yes she's [(laugh)
4.  J                        [(laugh)
5.  R      yes cos she (.) cos she goes down to the little house quite frequently
6.         now
```

These examples all indicate that a 'good' participant should fit into the research timetable easily and be available whenever necessary.

As a result of my initial conversation with Marie and speaking to women who had participated previously, I also contacted some women with whom I had not been in touch before. Marie suggested Kate and Rebecca, who became my next two recruits. They in turn offered several more names of women who might be interested. I decided that it was particularly important for the second stage of research that I should recruit participants who were closely connected to talk together about their photographs. This would generate the type of intimate, everyday talk I was looking for. To this end I made considered selections from the names suggested to me by the first recruits and the women I had previously spoken to. Kitty and Ethel from the previous study would have fitted into the group very well: but in their absence I had to consider others. Two others from the original research group had also agreed to take part in this piece. These were Helen, and Ellen who was Marie's sister and my aunt.

Helen readily agreed and I considered her to be particularly suitable as a partner in the second stage for Marie because they have been friends for over twenty years. This gave me one pairing of women, another being Kate and Rebecca, who are also long-standing friends and neighbours:

```
1.  K      seemed to become (.) oh (.) poor Mike was poorly and we seemed to
2.         become friendly that way I=
3.  J                               =mm (1) how long have you known each
4.         other then
5.  K      about twenty years cos we've lived here twenty years
```

My next contact was with Stella, who had been suggested by both Marie and Kate. Once I had obtained her agreement, I needed to recruit a suitable partner for her. A woman who none of them had suggested, but who I thought would be a possible candidate, was to become my sixth recruit. This was Millicent, a friend of Stella and also Marie's sister-in-law. She had connections to others in the group and so was closely linked to the network as a whole.

Following this my final two participants were added. Ellen willingly agreed to take part and she suggested that I should ask her friend Audrey who was also known both to Marie and myself. This suggestion was very useful because again Ellen and Audrey had been friends for many years:

```
1.   E      yeah but we started (1) gosh Audrey it was (1) y'see I didn't know
2.          Audrey until seventy (2) what was it Audrey
3.   A      seventy eight (.) [seventy seven
4.   E                        [seventy seventy seven seventy six or (.) round about
5.          that because she moved (.) y'know when we started when she came to
6.          work at Ratty's
```

Audrey's positive response meant that I had my final pair of co-conversationalists. Thus in the first part of the research I spoke to all eight women individually, and in the second part I spoke to pairings of Kate and Rebecca, Helen and Marie, and Ellen and Audrey[3]. This specific sample of women determined the data that was generated. The wide variety of conversations were a result of the particular co-conversationalists taking part. Certain topics were developed in detail in the talk whilst others were raised but not pursued. The conversational environment I had hoped for made possible the mundane, everyday interactions that I was interested in. As anticipated, the participants' shared knowledge was highlighted in the ways the pairs talked about the people they both knew, and in the ways people known to only one or other of them were introduced and discussed.

PARTICIPANT BIOGRAPHIES

Table 2.1 illustrates some of the biographical information given during the course of the conversations. The women are listed in the order in which I spoke to them, with myself at the end. The table helps to demonstrate the value of having in depth information about participants, particularly when researching relationships.

---

3 The planned 'paired' conversation between Stella and Millicent could not take place because soon after her participation in the first stage Stella's husband Don became seriously ill.

Table 2.1 Biographies

Name	Marital status	Children/Grandchildren
Kate (74)	married to Bert (82)	1 son who has lived in South Africa since 1974
Rebecca	was married to Mike; widowed since 1989	1 son with 3 children under 5 and 1 daughter with 2 children
Helen	divorced from Peter ten years ago	3 married sons and 3 grandchildren
Millicent	married to Pat	2 sons, 1 daughter and 6 grandchildren
Marie	married to Bill	3 daughters, 2 sons and 7 grandchildren
Stella	married to Don	1 son who died in 1989, 1 daughter and 2 grandchildren
Ellen	divorced from Ben in 1978	1 son in England, 1 daughter in U.S.
Audrey	married to Roy	2 sons, both living abroad, and 2 grandsons
Jane (44)	split up from Gary	2 daughters (1 pregnant) and 1 son

My discussion here of these relationships is concise and there is much more that I could have incorporated: but it provides a useful illustration of the extra information that can be gleaned from a qualitative examination of a relationship network, in conversation.

One of the central tenets of conversation analysis work is that nothing should appear in the analysis that is not present within the data – the only items significant to the analysis are those made relevant within the conversation by the co-conversationalists (Sacks, Schegloff and Jefferson 1974). The information presented in the above table is taken directly from the data set though it does not appear in the context that it was spoken – instead I am presenting my own personal 'take' on the biography of each of the women. From the wealth of biographical information talked about in the conversations – friends, work, places lived and so on – I have chosen to present family connections here as a detail that was included by all of the women when talking about their relationships. Whereas much biographical information varied between the women – for instance Kate and Ellen talked in detail about their various moves around the country and Marie and Millicent included long accounts of their childhood experiences – the family details of marriage, children and grandchildren were present in all of our conversations.

Though these family connections appeared consistently, the table presents a very simplified version of the variety of detail given, some of which seems to take on added importance within the table. One of the topics discussed by all of the women was their marital status but it is apparent from the table that the type of detail given about this varied. For instance, whereas none of the married women said for how long they had been married, Rebecca said how long she had been widowed and Helen and Ellen how long they had been divorced. Jane, the only other conversationalist who was not married, did not state the length of her separation. The reason for this exception is not apparent from the table, but it can be explained by examining the detail of the conversation – the context in which the information is given. From the context it becomes clear that the extra information given by Rebecca, Helen and Ellen was prompted by the questions Jane asked. For example to Rebecca:

1. J   so how long have you been on your own then (.) how long have you
2.   been a widow
3. R   err since eighty nine (.) nineteen eighty nine yes

However, in her role as researcher the lack of extra detail in Jane's account is not exceptional – during the course of the conversation Jane's biographical details are not always brought into focus in the same way as those of the other participants. This discrepancy illustrates the problematic nature of taking on the dual identities of both researcher and researched. In this case Jane's account is given in response to a disclosure from Helen about her own divorce. Jane follows with:

1. J   no cos I yeah cos when me and Gary who I'm going out
2.   with on Sunday night for a meal (laugh)
3. H   oh I've heard about this meal
4. J   when we split up y'know it was like it wasn't a shock
5.   because we just argued all the time

This response can be considered commonplace in the norms of ordinary conversation – it is quite usual for a personal disclosure from one person to be followed with something similar from another (Sacks 1992). However, in her identity as researcher it would be less commonplace for Jane to be the initiator of personal disclosure.

Another difference, again apparent from column two in the table, is that the names of all of the women's husbands and ex-husbands are given at some point in the conversations. What is not detailed, however, is that all of the men are named by their wives or ex-wives, apart from Mike who was married to Rebecca. Whenever she refers to him it is only as 'my husband', for example:

```
1.  J       who were the most influential people do you feel i'th'that you've (1) had
2.          relation[ships with
3.  R             [ships with (.) oh=
4.  J                           =during your life=
5.  R                                    =oh my goodness what a
6.          question
7.          (.) erm when my husband was alive obviously it was him
```

His name finally appears mid way through the conversation between Kate and Rebecca about their photographs, when he appears in a photograph of a past family party and Kate introduces his name in the course of telling how she met Rebecca.

A second aspect of the family biography discussed by all of the women at one time or another was their children and grandchildren. Some photographs showed them at various stages in their lives and particular details –their ages, marriages, occupations, and so on – were talked about in detail, whereas others were only talked about in passing. A large part of each of the conversations featured these varying aspects of their children's lives and the demands they still placed on the women even though they were all now grown up. It was notable that talk about their children by all of the women included information about where they lived. This topic was introduced in various ways. For instance Rebecca debated whether she should move to be nearer to them:

```
1.  R       I should move to be nearer the children er I think oh oh y'know=
2.  J                                                           =but
3.  J       they're at different ends of the country anyway [(laugh)
4.  R                                            [so yes (.) yes
5.  J       you'd have to move into the middle wouldn't you
```

Kate, on the other hand, talked in detail about visits she and her husband had made to South Africa to see her son who has lived there since 1974. She talked about some of the experiences they've had:

1. K   oh I've seen several snakes I just stand there and I saw a (.) erm last
2.   time we were there I saw a night adder went across the road in front of
3.   me at er (2) Charters Creek or somewhere I can't remember what it wa-
4.   I don't know what to do I just stand still and say 'look at that' or
                             [something like that
5. J   [mmmm
6. R   [(laugh) help
7. K   the man says to me 'where's it gone to' I said well it went in that grass
                                    there

Ellen too has a child who lives abroad – her daughter lives in the United States and is married to an American. Ellen visits regularly and said about her daughter:

1. E   she'll never ever come back and live in England
2. J   no
3. E   she's still British passport and everything but [erm
4. J   [how long has she been
5.   over there now
6. E   she left in eighty four love=

Another, more mundane topic of conversation related to children was the similar interests that they share. For instance Stella talks about the day-to-day activities she enjoys with her daughter and grandchildren such as:

1. S   yeah (.) our Beverley came with us as well [actually it's a good job she
                                  did=
2. J   [yeah
3. S   =because er::rm (1) ahh it's a long time well I mean sh- Shelley's twelve
4.   now she buys (1) different sort of clothes to what she used to do last time
5.   I took her shopping for clothes

Millicent on the other hand talks at length about her son who has recently returned to his wife after a lengthy split and the issues that the family members have encountered surrounding this move:

1. M   he's old enough to know what he's doing
2. J   well you would hope that he's old enough to know what he's doing

3.		although I don't know if that actually works
4.	M	yeah that's what Lesley's told Lesley says 'oh it's his life let him
5.		get on with it' leave it to 'em

A third aspect that became more obvious in constructing the table was that Kate was the only one of the participants to state her age during the conversation. This occurred during a stretch of talk about her husband having a pulmonary embolism, which she linked to his advanced age. When Jane expressed her surprise at this disclosure she then added her own age:

1.	K	no he's not having another operation but he he he can't fly he's had two
2.		pulmonary embolisms and [(.) erm we have to be careful=
3.	J	[right =yeah oh yeah
4.	K	well 'n he is eighty two (laugh)
5.	J	is he really
6.	K	yes
7.	J	oh crikey (laugh) that was your husband outside
8.	K	yes I'm sevent I'm seventy four
9.	J	you're not
10.	K	yes

Though none of the other women actually stated their age directly as Kate did, in some parts of the conversations their age at the time or event being talked about was given. This made it possible to work out with reasonable accuracy the age of the woman who is talking or being talked about. Jane's exact age was also known, but in contrast to Kate she did not volunteer her own age; instead it was introduced by Marie during her conversation with Helen and Jane in which Jane was compared to a photograph of Marie's grandma.

1.	M	she was forty but doesn't she look old d'y'think they d-
2.	H	no I don't think particularly there she does Marie
3.	M	yes but Jane's forty four

As with the discussion of divorce/separation given above, the disclosure of this information can be linked to the different identities that Jane has within the conversations. As a 'researcher' – with an aim of being objective – it is conventionally thought inappropriate to disclose personal information. However as a 'participant' it is completely acceptable for this type of information to be introduced and discussed within a conversation between friends.

CONCLUSION

In this paper I have given a brief outline of some of my experiences in recruiting and talking to this group of older women. The recruitment process was influenced and guided, not only by my own knowledge and previous experience, but also in large part by the women themselves. Their suggestions helped select the final members of the group. Through this selection I obtained many hours of very rich data, both in talk about long-term relationships and the relationships between the co-conversationalists which can be seen to be constructed and developed in a myriad of ways. In addition, the successful use of 'purposeful conversation' and discussion of personal photographs was made possible through these existing connections between the participants and myself. This rich volume of data enabled me to meet my original intention in this research to move the focus of relationship research from the general to the specific through a micro-analytic examination of how we construct our relationships in the details of our conversations. The very particular and selective process of recruitment to the research was crucial to this outcome.

Transcription notation

(.)	– a pause measuring less than one tenth of a second
(0.5)	– a pause measured in tenths of seconds
( )	– unclear stretches of talk
o:::old	– an extended sound
[	– overlapping utterances are marked by brackets at the beginning
[ ]	– simultaneous utterances are marked by brackets at the beginning and end
y- yeah	– a halting or cut off sound
(huh)	– laughter or other sounds appear within parentheses
=	– contiguous talk
=	

(adapted from Jefferson 1984)

REFERENCES

Burgess, R. (1988) Conversations with a purpose: the ethnographic interview in educational research, in R. Burgess (ed.) *Studies in Qualitative Methodology: A Research Annual.* London: Jai Press Inc, pp. 137–156.

Coupland, N., Coupland, J. and Giles, H. (1991) *Language, Society and the Elderly: Discourse, Identity and Ageing*. Oxford: Blackwell.

Ickes, W. (2000) Methods of studying close relationships, in W. Ickes and S. Duck (eds) *The Social Psychology of Personal Relationships.* Chichester: John Wiley and Sons, pp. 157–180.

Ickes, W. and Duck, S. (eds) (2000) *The Social Psychology of Personal Relationships*. Chichester: John Wiley and Sons.

Jefferson, G. (1984) Transcription notation, in J. M. Atkinson and J. Heritage (eds) *Structures of Social Action: Studies in Conversation Analysis*. Cambridge: Cambridge University Press, pp. ix–xvi.

Kanuha, V. K. (2000) 'Being' native versus 'going native': conducting social work research as an insider. *Social Work* 45(5): 439–447.

Miell, D. and Dallos, R. (eds) (1996) *Social Interaction and Personal Relationships*. London: Sage Publications.

Montague, J. and Stokoe, E. H. (1998) The conversational construction of older women's relationships: context, time and development. Paper presented at the British Psychological Society Women and Psychology Annual Conference, University of Birmingham.

Plummer, K. (2001) *Documents of Life 2: An Invitation to a Critical Humanism*. London: Sage.

Prosser, J. and Schwarz, D. (1998) Photographs within the sociological research process, in J. Prosser (ed.) *Image-based Research: A Sourcebook for Qualitative Researchers*. London: Falmer Press, pp. 115–130.

Radley, A. and Taylor, D. (2003) Images of recovery: a photo-elicitation study on the hospital ward. *Qualitative Health Research* 13(1): 77–99.

Rose, G. (2003) Family photographs and domestic spacings: a case study. *Transactions of the Institute of British Geographers* 28(1): 5–18.

Sacks, H. (1992) *Lectures on Conversation: Vols. I and II (Edited by Gail Jefferson)*. Oxford: Blackwell.

Sacks, H., Schegloff, E. A. and Jefferson, G. (1974) A simplest systematics for the organisation of turn taking for conversation. *Language* 50: 697–735.

Watson, R. (1997) Some general reflections on 'categorization' and 'sequence' in the analysis of conversation, in S. Hester and P. Eglin (eds) *Culture in Action: Studies in Membership Categorization Analysis.* Washington D.C.: International Institute for Ethnomethodology and Conversation Analysis and University Press of America, pp. 49–75.

3

RECRUITING OLDER RESEARCH PARTICIPANTS
Lessons from deprived neighbourhoods

THOMAS SCHARF [1]

INTRODUCTION

Even under the most favourable circumstances, recruiting older people to take part in social research can represent a major challenge for social gerontologists. Alongside more traditional concerns relating to the generation of sufficiently large sample sizes from which to generalise findings or securing the participation of people who meet a purposive sampling strategy, researchers are increasingly faced with the demands that arise from a commitment to involve older people themselves in different stages of the research process. These and related issues are explored here within the context of a study that had a potentially less favourable starting point.

Supported by the ESRC's Growing Older Programme, a research group at Keele University set out to examine aspects of the quality of life and social exclusion experienced by older people living in areas often regarded as difficult by social researchers – socially deprived neighbourhoods of three English cities. This chapter is divided into four main parts. First, it outlines the aims and intended methodology of the research project, which involved both quantitative and qualitative components. Second, it identifies several difficulties that arose in relation to implementing the proposed methodology, with a particular focus on the role of research ethics committees. Third, it highlights the way in which the research group sought to overcome these difficulties by rethinking its recruitment and sampling strategy. Fourth, the chapter concludes with some considerations for researchers embarking on similar empirical studies.

1 The research described in this article was supported by the Economic and Social Research Council's Growing Older Programme (Grant No. L480254022). Chris Phillipson, Allison Smith and Paul Kingston are to be acknowledged for their considerable contribution to this project.

THE RESEARCH PROJECT

The research set out to generate new insights into the experience of inequality in later life, examining a range of issues relevant to the quality of life of older people living in areas of intense social deprivation and seeking to develop understanding of factors contributing to social inclusion and exclusion in later life (Scharf et al. 2001, 2002a, 2002b). In broad terms, the aims were to:

- Contribute to knowledge about the circumstances of older people living in areas of concentrated poverty.
- Explore how older people manage their daily lives in deprived urban environments.
- Develop research methods relevant to studying quality of life issues for older people living in areas of concentrated poverty.
- Identify forms of deprivation which have yet to be addressed fully in gerontological and social policy research.
- Examine the dynamics of social exclusion at a neighbourhood level, and the implications of this for social policy.

A range of methodological approaches were proposed in order to meet these aims. The first stage involved identifying appropriate study areas in which to conduct a programme of empirical research. Liverpool, Manchester and the London Borough of Newham were selected on the basis of their ranking in the – then most current – official area deprivation measure.[2] To account for the substantial spatial variation that exists within these cities in relation to the intensity of deprivation, the research was concentrated on the three most deprived electoral wards in each city. All nine wards were ranked among England's 50 most deprived wards in 1998 (table 3.1).

To develop the research group's understanding of scientifically contested themes such as 'quality of life' and 'social exclusion', field research began with a series of discussions with groups of older people in the selected study areas. These discussions gave the research group the opportunity to raise with older people some of the emerging themes of the research project (Scharf et al. 2001) and a central feature was the attempt to find a form of words that potential research participants could identify

---

2 The Index of Local Deprivation (DETR, 1998) ranks communities according to their level of deprivation across 12 indicators, such as the unemployment rate, the number of Income Support recipients, standardised mortality rates and households lacking basic amenities.

Table 3.1 Study areas

Ward name	Local Authority district	Ward's ranking on 1998 deprivation index
Granby	Liverpool	4
Clubmoor	Liverpool	7
Longsight	Manchester	16
Cheetham	Manchester	17
Pirrie	Liverpool	20
Moss Side	Manchester	38
Park	Newham	42
Plashet	Newham	46
St Stephens	Newham	50

Source: DETR (1998)

with. Here we could consider the degree to which older people themselves responded to such concepts as social exclusion and quality of life. In all, seven groups were identified through contacts with relevant local agencies and existing local contacts. In addition and for the sake of comparison, a further group was held in a more affluent part of central England, and where appropriate, separate discussions took place with older people belonging to different ethnic groups. The groups ranged from the more formal (a pensioners forum with an agenda and a structured organisation) to the fully informal (a group of friends meeting in a hired church hall).

Two more intensive phases of fieldwork – representing the core feature of the research project – were to follow. The first was to involve a survey of 600 people aged 60 and over in the selected study areas. The purpose of this was to collect, first, socio-demographic data about the circumstances of older people living in deprived areas and, second, information relating to the themes of social exclusion and quality of life, including:

- characteristics of poverty and its impact on daily life;
- networks (including support networks) of older people;
- patterns of support within the older population and with other social groups;

- quality of life of older people (using standardised measures of physical and psychological well-being);
- characteristics of social participation within deprived localities;
- experiences of the urban environment in relation to services, crime, transportation and related issues.

The second phase of fieldwork involved conducting 130 semi-structured, in-depth interviews. Ninety interviews were to be undertaken with people who had previously taken part in the survey and agreed to be contacted again, and 40 with older people belonging to key minority groups in two of the study areas. These interviews sought to build upon the survey data but give greater emphasis, first, to the meaning of quality of life to older people living in deprived areas and, second, to variations in the experiences of sub-groups within the older population (ethnic minority groups, lone older people, people living in poverty). The interviews would explore in greater detail issues such as: experiences of daily life, strategies for survival in urban areas, the management of household finances, and social relationships within deprived localities.

In many respects, the proposed study might appear unremarkable. The research adopted a classic mixed methods design, and its methodology sought to build upon standard, tried-and-tested approaches that had worked in earlier projects (see, for example, Phillipson et al. 2001). However, several difficulties arose primarily in relation to the key task of recruiting older people to the fieldwork stages of the study.

PROPOSED RECRUITMENT STRATEGY: EMERGING DIFFICULTIES

The specific nature of the study – examining the circumstances of a particular age-group in a clearly defined geographic area in as representative a way as possible – suggested that general practitioner (GP) patient registers would be an appropriate means of recruiting older people to the research. Such lists have at least three major advantages for researchers in gerontology. First, the overwhelming majority of older people are registered with a GP, providing the necessary foundation for generating a representative sample. Second, the registers contain relevant information on the age and gender of patients, and thereby the potential to generate a stratified sample. Third, the registers are kept reasonably up-to-date. However, given the personal nature of the information contained within GP registers, a number of restrictions are necessarily placed on their use, and access to patient registers is safeguarded by Local Research Ethics Committees (LRECs).

To gain access to GP registers, the project team was required to negotiate its way through four such ethics committees (one of the research areas crossed two administrative boundaries at the time of application). What follows is a summary of some of the main difficulties experienced in securing such access. This story is likely to be familiar to other researchers who have embarked upon a recruitment strategy that involves accessing GP registers.

The process

Seeking ethical approval for research from LRECs usually requires completion of a range of relevant documentation. Even at an early stage of the research process, social scientists are likely to be confronted by a system that appears to lack direct relevance to their work. For example, forms will typically ask such questions as: 'Who is the clinical contact responsible for the care of your research subjects?' or 'When two or more methods of treatment are being compared, what criteria will be employed for deciding the point at which treatment is declared the preferred option and the research terminates?' On balance, though time-consuming, this part of the LREC process is usually straightforward. Application forms can generally be downloaded and completed electronically, and ethics committees publicise the details of submission deadlines and meeting dates well in advance. Moreover, we would also support the ethical principles underlying much of the documentation – for example, the requirement to secure informed consent, the need to avoid causing harm to research participants, and the importance attached to considering potential safety issues for research staff.

Perhaps rather less straightforward for social scientists is understanding the response of some LRECs to aspects of one's submission for ethical approval and what can appear to be a fundamental lack of understanding on the part of some LRECs of the nature of social science enquiry. Three examples illustrate this point:

1) *Sampling strategy*. Some committees took issue with the proposed approach to sampling. Despite our emphasis that the study was not to be – and indeed could not be – a randomised controlled trial, this feature of the research design was generally regarded negatively, leading one committee to demand a sample size calculation: 'A sample

size calculation must be supplied, stating clearly the nature and degree of expected differences to be subject to statistical analysis'. Re-emphasising that social science examines its data in a different way to the natural sciences had little impact on this particular committee, which responded that: 'The analysis should be planned prospectively and not as a reaction to emerging data and we would want to see ... details of the nature of statistical support (i.e. who helped with the analysis plan)'. Other committees questioned the absence of control groups.

2) *Scientific basis*. At times, LRECs appeared to reach beyond their formal powers to question the scientific merits of our research. This is particularly galling given the intense process of peer review that social scientists generally experience in securing funding for their research. As a minor example, one committee asked for 'clarification as to how social exclusion will be assessed'. Another sought 'reassurance that the research workers are experienced interviewers and experienced in the collection and analysis of qualitative data'. A different committee put it more bluntly: 'We believe that the sponsoring organisation [ESRC] may have conducted a scientific review and we would like to see copies of the referees' comments'. Linked to ideas more familiar to the natural than social sciences were a series of statements about the need to use a 'validated questionnaire'. In our view, such comments had relatively little to do with ethics and more to do with questioning the foundations of social scientific enquiry.

3) *Qualitative methods*. Some ethics committees view qualitative research methods in a distinctly negative light – as revealed in comments relating to the qualitative phase of our proposed research. A good example of deep-seated concerns arises from the concessions sought by some LRECs in relation to the data generated through in-depth interviews. In particular, the research group was asked to adapt consent forms to ensure that research participants were aware that tapes and transcripts of interviews would be destroyed. For example, one committee insisted on the following statement as part of its written consent form: 'I understand that should any information I give be tape-recorded, this information may be transcribed. The tape itself will be destroyed immediately after transcription'. Other LRECs required an open-ended commitment to destroy the tapes and transcripts after the end of the project. This type of requirement

naturally raises concerns for qualitative researchers who wish to establish and maintain a closeness to their data. It would deprive researchers of the opportunity to return to the original data at some future time, denying them the chance to reflect critically on initial interpretations of the data. Moreover, the destruction of tapes and transcripts seriously undermines the efforts of a social science community to build up an archive of qualitative data to match that which already exists in relation to quantitative data.[3]

Recruitment of research participants

The concerns outlined above tend to reflect a lack of awareness within some ethics committees of established research methods in the social sciences. As such, they represent minor irritations that can often be overcome by persuasive argument in favour of social research principles and techniques. Our experience was that a response that was robust yet reasonable tended to yield the required result. However, we found the ways that some LRECs sought to alter the basic methodology of the planned research considerably more difficult to cope with. In this case, the major sticking point related to the manner by which older people were to be recruited to the survey phase of the research.

All the LRECs initially opposed our preferred recruitment method. This was to invite people to participate in the research by letter, with a detailed information sheet attached. Unless potential participants opted-out of the study at this point, we suggested that the team could proceed to contact them again. The ethics committees universally opposed this recruitment strategy, favouring instead an opt-in procedure. This would require the research team to work through GPs to contact potential participants detailing the nature of the research. Only those older people who responded positively [in writing] to this request could then be recruited to the study.

From the perspective of the research group, the nature of the planned study meant that it was unthinkable to accept such an opt-in strategy. People agreeing to opt-in would differ substantially from the population of older people in deprived areas as a whole, thus generating a significant source of sample bias. As we argued to the LRECs, the opt-in procedure would tend to generate a sample composed of people who were relatively

---

3 Details of the ESDS Qualidata archive, are available online at: http://www.esds.ac.uk/introduction.asp

young, of above-average social status, in better physical and mental health, of a higher standard of education, and who belonged to majority ethnic groups. By contrast, many of the very people whose quality of life and risk of social exclusion we were interested in assessing would be excluded from the research process: people who were older, of lower social status, in poorer health, who had lower levels of education and who belonged to minority ethnic groups. In effect, the opt-in procedure would provide such a distorted sample that the research findings would not present an accurate reflection of local circumstances, let alone be generalisable to other areas of England characterised by high levels of social deprivation.

The research group also felt that the opt-in procedure was open to criticism on ethical grounds. Were such a procedure to be adopted in this and similar studies, a significant population group might be lost to any type of social research. In this respect, the views of an already marginalised group of older people would be absent from research, potentially increasing their risk of marginalisation. Given the current health and social policy focus on tackling inequalities and neighbourhood deprivation (Social Exclusion Unit 1998, 2001), the absence of a voice from groups such as older people in deprived areas could potentially lead to inappropriate and ill-founded policy outcomes for these groups. In our view, this point was potentially compounded by the considerable variation that marks the practice of LRECs across England. While some committees appeared to adhere doggedly to an 'opt-in' procedure in sample recruitment, others ultimately proved willing to accept a suitably framed 'opt-out' approach. We argued that the outcome of such a disparity would be an inclination amongst scientists to undertake research in localities where the 'opt-out' procedure prevails. This is an undesirable situation, since it means that particular locations and their populations would be under-researched – perhaps even becoming no-go areas for social research – while other areas and their residents would tend to be over-researched.

On the basis of the arguments presented by the research team, it proved possible to convince two of the four LRECs concerned of the merits of an opt-out recruitment procedure. This was a major achievement. However, despite a number of approaches and attempts at addressing specific concerns that might arise from an opt-out procedure, the other two committees refused to shift from their insistence on an opt-in recruitment strategy.

RETHINKING RECRUITMENT: AN ALTERNATIVE APPROACH TO SAMPLING

Generating a random sample

At this stage – ten months after having made initial contact with the LRECs – the research group faced a fundamental problem. If recruitment to the survey differed from study area to study area, this would seriously compromise the research team's ability to report emerging findings. Unwilling to accept this limitation, alternative recruitment strategies were considered. The option of knocking on doors and undertaking a household census in selected streets within the study areas represents a potential means of generating a usable sampling frame. This was rejected on the grounds of resource limitations, the potential safety risks that would arise for cold-calling fieldworkers, and the distinct likelihood of failure (many older people who took part in the initial discussion groups told the research team that they were unlikely to open their front door to strangers).

In the end, a solution to the sampling problems was found through an unlikely route. Drawing on the expertise of a commercial data management company (CACI Ltd), the research team made use of an innovative classificatory method that places people into a series of 15 five-year age bands and 21 age types according to their first names. The classification (known by the acronym MONICA) is based on a combination of anonymous Census data and a sample of real birth registrations dating from 1900. Each first name is associated with a median age which identifies the statistical likelihood that someone with that name will belong to a particular age group. When applied to electoral registers, this approach is able to generate a random list of names and addresses of people likely to match specific age requirements.[4] A sampling frame was generated that included all of the Ethels and Stanleys that lived in the chosen study areas, whilst ignoring the modish Kylies and Jasons and the more timeless Elizabeths and Johns (table 3. 2).

The sampling frame included the names and addresses of 2,302 people potentially aged 60 and over in nine electoral wards (table 3.3). Of these names and addresses, 1,116 were subsequently deemed ineligible for a variety of reasons. A number of people had moved house or died. As anti-

---

4 Further details are available online at: http://www.caci.co.uk.

Table 3.2 MONICA – examples of names

Men	Women	Median age
Baden	Agnes	65.8
Cedric	Dilys	65.8
Edward	Eileen	65.8
Arthur	Ernestine	72.5
Leonard	Nancy	72.5
Reginald	Vera	72.5
Archie	Bessie	76.6
Lancelot	Florence	76.6
Wilfred	Maude	76.6

Table 3.3 Sample recruitment

	Number	Percent
Selected addresses	2,302	100
Ineligible addresses	1,116	48
Eligible addresses	*1,186*	*52*
Refusals	360	30
Non-contact	325	27
Interviews achieved	**501**	**42**

cipated, a significant minority were of the wrong age, and others were too ill to participate. Of the 1,186 potentially eligible respondents, 360 refused to participate and – despite up to five attempts on different days and at different times of the day – 325 could not be contacted. A total of 501 interviews were completed, giving a response rate of 42 per cent.

The fact that the research was able to generate a random sample drawn in the same way from the electoral registers of each ward, and subsequently complete a survey of people in the required age-group, provides an indication of the utility of this recruitment strategy and its potential for future gerontological work. The research team also felt that this approach may ultimately prove more ethically sound than the use of GP patient registers, given that people do not generally register with GPs in the expectation that personal data will potentially be passed on to social researchers.

Generating a purposive sample

One obvious drawback with the MONICA classification system is that it generates a sample of people from particular cultural and ethnic backgrounds. In our research, we succeeded by this method in recruiting older people to the survey who were primarily white and English-speaking, or of Black Caribbean origin. However, one of the key features of the research project described here was to identify differences in relation to social exclusion and quality of life for different groups of older people, including people belonging to ethnic minorities. One of the difficulties associated with past research on ethnic minorities has been an inability to distinguish adequately between different groups of older people. Typically, a nationally or locally representative survey of older people would yield too few people from particular minority groups to facilitate analysis according to an ethnicity variable. One way around this problem might be the 'pooling' of data from successive years or waves of a survey (as undertaken by Evandrou 2000), but this is rarely possible and not always satisfactory. An alternative strategy – well-suited to community-based studies – is to draw research participants from particular minority groups. In our project, a decision was made to collect data from the numerically largest ethnic minority groups in each of the study areas. Somali people in Liverpool, Pakistani people in two Manchester wards, additional Black Caribbean people in a third Manchester ward, and Indian people in Newham were targeted in this research as a way of generating sufficient cases to allow at least a basic level of analysis according to ethnicity. The advantages of such an approach were felt to outweigh any disadvantages associated with the use of two different sampling systems. In particular, by gathering sufficient data from people in a select range of groups it would be possible to comment on the specific nature of social exclusion and disadvantage affecting older people from different backgrounds.

Recruiting older people from specific minority groups into research programmes tends to occur in a purposive way, largely through the development of contacts with local organisations and snowballing techniques. In our research, we were able to build upon existing links with groups within the study communities to generate the different samples. However, this is never straightforward, especially when dealing with different groups in each study area. There is inevitably some resistance within minority groups to participating in research that appears to have no obvious benefit to the community. Whilst supporting the need for research, group representatives and professionals working with minorities often comment on the lack of feedback from researchers to research participants. Overcoming cynicism about the motives of researchers is therefore an important first step in securing access. In our research, progress was made by:

- seeking to convince gate-keepers that the absence of recent research might limit the minority groups' ability to influence policy;
- recruiting fieldworkers from the relevant groups and, through appropriate training, developing individuals' skills in social research;
- maintaining regular formal and informal contacts with relevant community organisations and individuals;
- agreeing to feedback the findings from our research in a variety of ways.

In all, ninety-nine people were recruited from black and minority ethnic groups using a purposive sampling strategy.

Ensuring successful recruitment

The success of the major fieldwork stage of the research described here can also be attributed to a range of other tried-and-tested strategies used to recruit people to social research projects. For example, great care was taken over initial letters of invitation (all 2,302 were personally addressed and signed) and the preparation of an accessible information sheet. Members of the research group were available – through telephone, post and email – to answer questions that older people or their relatives might have about the nature of the proposed research. Fieldwork was undertaken by trained interviewers belonging to a commercial survey organisation (Marketing Sciences) that had previous experience of conducting work in similar types of geographic area. On completion of interviews, a leave-behind thank-you letter was accompanied by an information sheet highlighting a welfare advice service operated by Help the Aged.

All respondents who agreed to divulge their names and addresses to the research group as a precursor to taking part in a follow-up interview were also sent a copy of the next project newsletter. Whilst serving to keep people informed about the research, the newsletter also reminded people that they might be called upon to participate in the final stage of fieldwork. Recruitment to the in-depth interviews was made more straightforward by the fact that research participants had previously indicated their willingness to take part in a second interview, but it still proved necessary to convince people of the potential benefits of taking part. In this respect, we were helped by the development of a close link between the project and Help the Aged. With initial evidence from the survey pointing to the high rates of poverty and intense social disadvantage experienced by many older people in the study areas, the research group entered into a formal collaboration with the charity. Help the Aged subsequently published a 'user-friendly' report of the project's key findings (Scharf et al. 2002b). This report has since been used to influence public policy development, and – somewhat less directly – to feed findings back to research participants through a range of media. Thus, when recruiting people to the final stage of fieldwork, the research team sought to appeal not only to participants' altruistic nature, but also to show an active commitment to publicising our findings as widely as possible.

SUMMARY

This article has highlighted a range of practical problems associated with recruiting older people to take part in social research projects. Some of these problems are likely to be common to many empirical studies. Others assume added significance when research seeks to address the situation of people living in particular environmental settings. In particular, our research has drawn attention to the laborious and energy-sapping nature of seeking ethical approval from medically oriented Local Research Ethics committees. Though there are merits associated with seeking such formal approval for one's research – not least because engagement with the ethics process requires social gerontologists to become much clearer about the practicalities involved in their planned programme of field research – it is an experience that the author would be reluctant to repeat in future. While all recruitment and sampling strategies have their pitfalls, on balance our experience with the use of electoral registers and the classification of people's first names has been a positive one.

However, there are also dangers associated with abandoning GP patient registers as a suitable sampling frame for social research, raising a more general concern about the nature of studies undertaken by social gerontologists in Britain. An established and important type of social research – medium-scale surveys with a qualitative follow-up – are likely to become much less common unless better access to GP registers is offered. This applies especially to studies that have a relatively short duration (say, less than three years), since the requirement to secure ethical approval casts the entire research timetable into doubt. In place of this type of research will come studies based on the secondary analysis of large datasets, studies with self-recruiting samples, and qualitative research that draws upon purposive sampling strategies. As a result, particular social groups and geographic areas that are viewed in some way as being problematic might become under-represented in social science enquiry.

Finally, in reflecting on our experience during the different stages of this project, we would continue to argue in favour of increasing the degree to which a broad range of users are involved in research. Our initial commitment to engage with non-academic research users ultimately absorbed a considerable amount of time and effort. Indeed, this commitment has extended long beyond the period for which the research was funded. However, such engagement has been vital in helping the project team to develop new insights into the day-to-day experiences of older people living in socially deprived neighbourhoods of England. Without having adopted an inclusive strategy of involving participants in elements of the research, it is unlikely that the project would have generated the quantity and quality of data that has allowed us to present research findings in a way that holds the potential to improve the well-being of older people.

REFERENCES

DETR (1998) *Updating and Revising the Index of Local Deprivation*. London: Department of the Environment, Transport and the Regions.

Evandrou, M. (2000) Social inequalities in later life: the socio-economic position of older people from ethnic minority groups in Britain. *Population Trends*, Autumn, pp. 11–18.

Phillipson, C., Bernard, M., Phillips, J. and Ogg, J. (2001) *Family and Community Life of Older People*. London: Routledge.

Scharf, T., Phillipson, C., Kingston, P. and Smith, A. E. (2001) Social exclusion and ageing. *Education and Ageing* 16(3): 303–320.

Scharf, T., Phillipson, C., Smith, A. E. and Kingston, P. (2002a) Older people in deprived areas: perceptions of the neighbourhood. *Quality in Ageing* 3(2): 11–21.

Scharf, T., Phillipson, C., Smith, A. E. and Kingston, P. (2002b) *Growing Older in Socially Deprived Areas: Social Exclusion in Later Life.* London: Help the Aged.

Social Exclusion Unit (1998) *Bringing Britain Together: A National Strategy for Neighbourhood Renewal.* London: Stationery Office.

Social Exclusion Unit (2001) *A New Commitment to Neighbourhood Renewal.* London: Stationery Office.

4

RECRUITING OLDER PEOPLE TO TALK ABOUT SEX
Some practical and theoretical reflections

REBECCA L. JONES

This chapter reflects on my experiences of recruiting older people to talk about sex. The research I discuss was a three-year PhD study funded by the School of Health and Social Welfare at the Open University, entitled 'Older women talking about sex: a discursive analysis' (Jones 2003). I report on some practical issues I encountered and the results of the recruitment processes I used. To give the context of these processes I discuss first, at a more theoretical level, some of the implications of asking older people to talk about sex, given the broader cultural resources about older people's sexuality that are available in 21st-century Britain.

RESEARCH AS CULTURALLY SITUATED

In common with other social constructionist researchers (e.g. Burr 1995; Gergen 1985), I understand academic research to be necessarily part of the wider cultural realm in which it is undertaken. I do not consider it to be possible for a research project or a researcher to stand neutrally outside the topic being investigated. Rather, research itself necessarily draws on broader cultural resources that are historically and culturally specific. An important task for the researcher, then, is to understand the ways in which their research has been shaped by these broader cultural resources. It is essential to identify and interrogate the prevalent ideas about a topic to be researched, since research projects themselves draw on or react to these ideas.

In this chapter, I call these common ideas 'cultural resources' in order to suggest their familiar and commonsensical character. These common ideas are historically and culturally specific but widely available. They are of interest not for the 'truth' or otherwise of the ideas described, but for the ways in which they are used and have social effects. In this section, my intention is to indicate the familiar commonsense quality that they have, rather than to specify their nature or content precisely. For more detailed discussion of the nature and workings of these cultural resources, see (Jones 2002, 2003). The cultural resources I describe in the following section are not the only ways in which it is possible to think about older people and sex, but they are particularly common ones.

CULTURAL RESOURCES ABOUT OLDER PEOPLE AND SEX

As many commentators have noted (Benbow and Jagus 2002; Greengross and Greengross 1989; Weg 1983) older people are often seen as asexual. Older people are excluded from many contexts where sex is at issue. Sexual health information and campaigns are targeted almost exclusively at younger people (with the exception of a few campaigns by older people's organisations). The major recent surveys of sexual behaviour in the UK – the *National Survey of Sexual Attitudes and Lifestyles* (Johnson et al. 2001; Wellings, Field, Johnson and Wadsworth 1994) – limited respondents to those aged under 59. The book that presents the findings of the 1990–91 version of this survey justifies the exclusion of older people from the study on several grounds. One of these is the claim that 'many of the topics for which data were collected are known not to affect older people greatly' (Wellings et al. 1994, p. 23). One wonders how it is known that these topics do not affect older people if they are excluded from surveys such as this.

A related but distinct cultural resource is the idea that sex in later life is disgusting and risible. Coupland (2000) reports that a storyline about older people and sex in the BBC's *EastEnders* soap-opera led to large numbers of letters of complaint from viewers. The two people were portrayed as in their early 60s and the scene showed only bare shoulders in bed but viewers used words such as 'revolting' and 'horrible' (ibid., p. 13). The expression 'dirty old man' is often used to describe any sexual activity or interest in an older man, often in situations where the same behaviour by a young man would be accepted or even valorised. The ageing body is often singled out as a source of this revulsion, and incontinence, wrinkles and sagging are often mentioned. For example, there is a genre of birthday cards that make jokes about the recipient's sex life now that they are older, including cartoon drawings of naked older people with exaggerated wrinkles and such props as zimmer frames and inflatable 'old lady' sex dolls.

A related but distinct idea is that older people cannot talk about sex. Questions about my research often centre on the presumed difficulties of obtaining data where older people talk about sex. People often ask me 'how on earth did you get them to talk about that?' and 'did you find that they had the vocabulary to talk about that sort of thing?' This idea is found in the academic literature as well as in everyday life. Deacon, Minichiello and Plummer (1995, p. 507) characterise as one of the difficulties in research design for any work on older people and sexuality that: 'older people may also be reluctant to speak candidly about their sexuality'. The idea that older people are unwilling or incompetent speakers about sex does not necessarily imply that older people do not have sex. However there is a potential link because older people might be thought to be unwilling to speak about sex because later life sex is deviant or because they have nothing to say because it is not pertinent to them.

These ideas that later life sexuality is non-normative are far from the only available cultural resources. The second half of the 20th-century saw the growth of an idea that older people may continue to be sexually active and interested. During the three-year period when I undertook this research there were at least half a dozen television programmes about older people and sex, and numerous articles in newspapers and magazines including those aimed at younger people (such as *Eve* magazine, 2001). Much academic research since the 1960s and especially since the 1980s has argued that many older people do continue to be sexually active and interested (e.g. Brecher 1984; Starr and Bakur 1981; Verwoedt, Pfeiffer and Wang 1969). These articles and programmes almost always frame what they are doing as breaking taboos, dispelling myths or disproving stereotypes about older people and sex. Older people who do talk about sex are often valorised as brave, honest or taboo-breaking. This framing extends to much of the academic and practitioner literature where it seems almost obligatory to use the structure 'people often think older people are asexual but this article dispels the myth'.

Having noticed the prevalence of this cultural resource, I wanted my own research to problematise it and not to take it for granted as the starting place for research about older people and sex. I did not want to reproduce the dominant academic and practitioner framing of the topic where older people talking about sex are treated as taboo-breaking and revelatory. It seemed to me that this emphasis on breaking taboos was itself a subtle form of ageism. Such a framing does not treat it as ordinary and everyday for older people to talk about sex. Rather, it treats older people talking about sex as exceptional and noteworthy. I wanted to undertake research where I did not take it for granted that there was anything special and noteworthy about older people talking about sex.

PROBLEMATISING CULTURAL RESOURCES

This led to a number of related prior questions. Firstly, is talking about sex special and noteworthy in general? Plummer (1995) has demonstrated that there are now whole genres of widely available sexual stories that speakers can draw on to talk about their own sexual experiences. While not all individuals have equal access to these resources for talking about sex and while not all types of sexual behaviour and identity are valued equally, it is certainly the case that talk about sex is very prominent in many parts of 21st-century British culture.

One of the ways in which talk about sex is often treated as exceptional and noteworthy is by framing it as a delicate or difficult topic. This suggested a second prior question; is sex inherently a delicate or difficult topic to talk about? Silverman's study of talk in HIV counselling interactions shows that treating sex as a delicate sensitive topic is one of the available culturally familiar ways of talking about sex but it is not inherent to the topic (Silverman 1997). As he discusses, routine professional talk by workers in a Genito-Urinary Medicine clinic does not treat sex as a delicate or sensitive topic. This suggests that the idea that talking about sex is a sensitive and delicate matter might tell us more about people's ideas about how sex *should* be talked about than about how it actually is talked about. In some contexts, it may be considered appropriate to treat sex as a sensitive topic, but in other contexts it may not be. This suggests that the sensitivity is associated with the context rather than with the topic of sex itself. As the researcher, I had some control over the context in which sex is talked about, since I would be setting up the meeting. This meant that I could endeavour to frame the topic in ways that did not assume its sensitivity.

If research about sex is framed as a sensitive, difficult topic, it is likely that researchers will find that people talk about sex in this way. Having concluded that talk about sex in general was not necessarily difficult and sensitive, I did not want to presume that the fact that I proposed to talk to *older people* about sex made it difficult and sensitive: I did not want to take it for granted that talking about sex was difficult for older people.[1]

---

1 There are, of course, a host of other reasons why talking about sex could have been difficult, including the generational difference between me and respondents. I discuss some of the effects of our generational difference elsewhere (Jones 2003). The point here is that I did not want to assume difficulty as a starting point for the interaction.

So I set out to try to recruit older people to take part in my research without assuming that it was a sensitive and difficult topic. However, in practice this proved to be very difficult on a number of different levels, as I now discuss.

THE DIFFICULTY OF TERMINOLOGY

One of the first problems I encountered was how to describe the topic of the research when inviting people to take part. 'Sex' is my own preferred shorthand for the phenomenon in which I am interested here, but there were a number of difficulties with using this term in my recruitment materials.

Firstly, the term is often used very narrowly to describe only physical sexual acts. Feminist and Queer theorists have shown that what is described as 'sex' is politically and culturally variable and is not a natural given (Bland and Mort 1997; Butler 1990; Jackson and Scott 1996; Rich 1980). This body of research has drawn attention to the importance of the context in which physical sexual acts occur, such as relationships, life stages and societal norms. My own understanding of the nature and meanings of sexual activity have been strongly shaped by this literature and this means that I understand sex to be about much more than physical sexual acts. Secondly, 'sex' is sometimes understood to mean heterosexual penetrative sex. I did not want to use a term that was likely to be understood in this way both because I did not want to exclude non-heterosexual older people and also because older people may be particularly likely to have non-penetrative forms of sex due to the physiological changes that commonly accompany ageing. Thirdly, I wanted to give respondents some degree of flexibility about how explicitly they talked. I wanted the topic of the research to sound broad enough to give respondents some scope for choosing what they actually talked about once they had met me and found out more about the research. Fourthly, and most practically, I was worried that if I put my own name and contact details next to the word 'sex' in public media such as newspapers and local radio, I might experience sexually harassing contacts.

These last two reasons demonstrate my own inability to frame the topic in a straightforward way that did not assume sensitivity. I would not have worried about giving respondents scope to talk at different levels of explicitness if I had not thought that the topic might be embarrassing to them. I would not have worried about a public association with sex if I was not drawing on the idea that public talk about sex made me vulnerable. That is not to say that I was wrong to draw on these ideas. It seems perfectly reasonable for researchers to do what they can to protect themselves from sexual harassment and to be aware of respondents' possible sensitivities. My point is that even at the very earliest stages of naming research about sex, difficulties arise in problematising common ways of understanding talk about sex because these common framings are very powerful and pervasive.

After an initial attempt to use the word 'sex' in recruiting respondents, described in the next section, I decided to use the phrase 'intimate relationships' instead. It quickly became apparent that most respondents understood this to be a straightforward euphemism for sex. For example, one woman told me that she had told a friend that I was coming to see her and her friend had said 'she'll ask you about sex and do you still know how to do it!' However, using terminology that is seen as euphemistic is one of the culturally familiar ways of dealing with difficult and sensitive topics. Thus, in yet another way, it became apparent me that I had ended up treating the topic as sensitive.

THE FRIENDSHIP CLUB

My first idea for a method that might create data where older people talked about sex was to run a discussion session at an existing older people's group. Through my previous work for an Age Concern organisation, I knew an older woman who was interested in my research and ran a Friendship Club. The club meets weekly and sometimes has invited speakers but more usually the members play bingo, chat and go on outings. We agreed that I should attend one meeting and run a workshop. I immediately hit a difficulty with my attempt not to assume that it was a sensitive issue. The organiser was the gatekeeper of my access to this group of older people and she did not want me to use the word 'sex' in describing what I was interested in. This was before I had the idea of using 'intimate relationships' and we came up with a compromise of 'relationships, intimacy and health as we grow older'.

On the day of my session seven members were present, six women and one man, aged between 60 and 90. I had prepared a series of vignettes about older people experiencing issues to do with sex and relationships, such as having a holiday romance; contracting a Sexually Transmitted Infection; experiencing sexual changes in a long-standing relationship when one partner had dementia; deciding whether to remarry; and finding out that a grandson was gay. I asked people in small groups to read two or three vignettes, to discuss them and then to describe the vignettes to the larger group and summarise their discussion. I tape recorded the whole session.

On transcribing the tape, it was apparent that there was very little talk about sex, even very broadly defined to include other aspects of relationships with sexual partners. There was some talk about sex in the small groups which I overheard at the time but this was not audible on the tape. When people were reporting back to the larger group they talked about issues around ageing and ageism, family relationships and societal change. The sexual content of the vignettes was glossed over and in some cases the transcript shows that the speaker is reading from the vignette but missing out the sentences that referred directly to sexual activity. One vignette did occasion particularly animated discussion in the small group. It concerned a woman who had a hysterectomy and felt afterwards that she was no longer 'a proper woman'. I picked up that one member, June,[2] had very strong feelings about the situation but I was unable to encourage her to elaborate on it. While it would perhaps be interesting to speculate about why they did not talk about things that I recognised as sex, the issue for me at the time was that the session had not generated the sort of data I wanted.

INDIVIDUAL INTERVIEWS

I therefore decided to try individual interviews as an alternative data gathering method. I went back to the Friendship Club and while the ordinary meeting was going on, individuals who wanted to, talked to me in another room. One of these interviewees was June. As soon as we sat down she said 'I want to tell you this' and told me about how traumatic it was when she had a hysterectomy. A large part of the trauma was that her husband was completely unsympathetic, refused to have sex with her and told her she was no longer a proper woman. It seemed that she thought it appropriate to talk much more explicitly and personally in an interview setting them she had during the discussion session. Perhaps to have told this story amongst her friends would be seen as being disloyal to her husband, to whom she is still married.

The idea that research interviews are a confidential, private space where personal talk is appropriate is a widely available one. I therefore decided to use one-to-one interviews as my main data-gathering method.

2 All names and other identifying details of respondents have been changed.

This worked very well and generated large amounts of data where older women talked about many aspects of sex in later life.

BENEFITS OF TREATING IT AS A SENSITIVE TOPIC

Somewhat reluctantly, I concluded that it was helpful to treat the topic of sex in later life as a sensitive and private issue that might be difficult to talk about. I drew on all the obvious ways of framing the topic that I had started out wanting to problematise. By stressing the anonymity and confidentiality of interviewees' contributions, I reinforced the notion that the topic was sensitive and private, since sensitive and private matters demand anonymity and confidentiality. In deciding to talk only to older women, I both drew on and perpetuated the idea that talking about sex is appropriately done between members of the same gender. By talking about sex in an interview setting, I added to the familiar notion that one-to-one interviews are an appropriate vehicle for talk about sex. As already described, I found that I was myself unable to step entirely outside the idea that sex was a sensitive topic.

However, this is not to say that treating sex as a sensitive topic prevented talk about sex in later life. Rather, it can be seen that there are significant benefits to framing the topic as sensitive and difficult and that these benefits actually function to enable such talk. If interviewees had not demonstrated an awareness of the sensitivity and riskiness of what they were talking about, they would have risked appearing strange, crass or rude. Similarly, if I had not displayed awareness of the sensitivity of the topic I might have appeared untrustworthy or insensitive. The idea that 'serious' talk about personal experiences of sex is a delicate topic is so prevalent that I would argue that speakers usually need to negotiate around it.

In the interviews, the women often invoked the idea of the sensitivity of talk about sex in later life at the same time as talking very explicitly about it. For example, Lesley had been talking about masturbating with her last sexual partner, told a joke that included the word 'wanker' and then added 'That's very rude I shouldn't be telling you that!' Similarly, Win frequently checked whether she was shocking me and emphasised how honest she was being in talking frankly to me about her sexual experiences. Discursive moves such as these can position the speaker as informed, rational, honest, truthful and as someone who sees beyond the conventional. Such moves also treat the research itself as important, original and interesting because it is thereby claimed that it is seeing beyond the conventional. This gives the research itself a superior truth claim. For a more detailed discussion of the benefits and workings of such discursive moves, see Jones (2002; 2003). Thus, treating talk about sex in later life as a delicate topic can carry significant benefits for the researcher, the respondents and the research project itself.

SOURCES OF INTERVIEWEES

In the remaining sections of this chapter, I describe briefly the results of my recruitment strategies and reflect on the ways in which these strategies affected the sort of data produced. I interviewed 23 women who responded to a variety of recruiting techniques. Several techniques produced only one respondent each (posters in local libraries, posters in local Age Concern offices, an Open University press release, and an interview on local radio). Two techniques produced two respondents each (an article in a local University of the Third Age newsletter and colleagues passing on fliers to their mothers-in-law). Two techniques produced four respondents each – an article in a local paper, and members of the Friendship Club and some of their friends. The single most successful source of respondents was a newsletter in the national Growing Old Disgracefully newsletter – this produced eight interviewees.[3] Thus, the most effective ways of recruiting interviewees were the article in the local paper, contact with the Friendship Club and the Growing Old Disgracefully newsletter. This latter was perhaps particularly successful because talking about and having sex in later life can easily be framed as part of the same project as 'growing old disgracefully'.

Recruitment techniques that did not produce any respondents were: flyers to staff and volunteers of a large local Age Concern Group; flyers through a national Age Concern network; posters in a Relate administrative office; posters in churches and community centres; and a handout to a Women's Institute group.

CHARACTERISTICS OF INTERVIEWEES

Interviewees can be briefly characterised in demographic terms. They were aged between 61 and 90; two-thirds of them were aged under 75 and one-third over 75. They lived all over England and several of them lived in Milton Keynes, London and Yorkshire. They all lived in their own homes and five of them lived in sheltered housing complexes. They came from a wide range of socio-economic backgrounds and those who had been formally employed had had jobs including market-trader, factory-worker, clerical assistant, nurse and teacher. The respondents recruited via the Growing Older Disgracefully network tended to be more middle-class and more educated than most of the other respondents. They were all 'white' and two specified that they were Jewish. Two described themselves as lesbians and one said that she thought she was probably bisexual although she had never had a relationship with a woman. One woman had been disabled all her life and several others were experiencing more recent disabilities.

In terms of their sexual and relationship histories, all the women had been in relatively long-term relationships (ten years or more, and many thirty years or more). Only three of the women were still in the same long-term relationship and those were the three currently married women in the group. None of these three were happy in that long-term relationship. All the women had been in relationships for the vast majority of their adult lives – there were no lifelong single people. Within the group there was a vast range of different experiences of sexual relationships. These included divorce (8 women); remarriage (5); never being married (2); widowhood (15); serial monogamy (15); relationships with two people at the same time (1); relationships where one partner is married to someone else (5); becoming a carer of a partner (8); domestic violence both now (1) and in the past (2); sexual abuse as a child (2); and the formation of new relationships after the age of 60 (9).

EFFECTS OF RECRUITMENT PROCESSES ON THE TALK IN THE INTERVIEWS

The recruitment processes affected the sort of people who took part in the research, as I have described above. I also analysed the posters, newsletter and newspaper articles which I used to recruit respondents, in order to see how they might have affected what was said in the interviews. There is of course no deterministic link between how an interview is set up and what is actually said in the event. However, analysing the recruitment processes can help the researcher to

---

3 These numbers add up to 24 because one woman said she had both read my article in the U3A newsletter and heard my interview on local radio.

understand some of the things they have been taking for granted about the research

All the documents contained assurances that contributions would be confidential and anonymous. This implies that participants have secrets with which they may not wish to be publicly associated, and that confidences may be told within the interview. In this way, the recruiting materials perpetuated the idea that intimate relationships in later life are a sensitive or delicate topic.

Several of the recruiting documents claimed that the research is important. This claim makes possible accounts where the subject is significant and serious, despite being about private and personal matters that are sometimes treated as insignificant and not noteworthy. It may also have excluded potential respondents who did not feel that they had something important to say. Most of the recruiting materials start with the question 'do you have something to say about intimate relationships in later life?' This invokes the idea that the accounts to be elicited are newsworthy: an emphasis that facilitates the telling of accounts in which participants have strong feelings, noteworthy experiences or firmly held beliefs. It perhaps makes less available other positions from which potential respondents might have spoken, such as benevolent disinterest or having nothing important to say.

Many of the recruiting materials made reference to wrong assumptions about older people and intimate relationships, for example 'lots of people assume that once you're past retirement age, you stop being interested in relationships and intimacy. Or they think that older people are too embarrassed to talk about these sorts of topics. But this isn't always true.' This phrase, which I used in the newsletter articles, implies that respondents know better than 'lots of people' and this facilitates accounts where interviewees do talk about their experiences of intimate relationships in later life. It also valorises both interviewer and interviewee because they know better than other people do. It seems likely that the talk about breaching norms, mentioned above, was facilitated by this framing before we even met.

CONCLUSION

One of my goals in undertaking this research was to problematise the very activity of recruiting older people to talk about sex. I wanted to think about what it meant to undertake research about this topic given the common cultural resources about older people and sex. Initially, I tried to avoid framing the topic as a sensitive or difficult one and tried to approach it in a straightforward and everyday manner. However, I ended up, somewhat reluctantly, treating the topic as both sensitive and delicate. This happened both because of initial difficulties in inducing the sort of accounts I was interested in and also because of my own culturally mediated awareness of the ways in which it is usually considered appropriate to talk about sex. Just as respondents draw on common ideas about what sort of topics are sensitive, so too the researcher is embedded in societal norms about ways of talking about sensitive topics and this meant that my own ability to step outside the framing of sex as a delicate topic was limited. However, this framing of sex as a delicate topic was not absolute and did not prevent talk about sex. Rather, as discussed above, it enabled talk about sex by positioning interviewees as taboo-breaking and particularly honest people who were telling the truth despite common ideas that older people do not have or talk about sex. It is not possible entirely to step outside powerful cultural resources about the sensitivity of talking about sex for people of any age. What the researcher can do, though, is to be reflexive about the ways in which different cultural resources are invoked and reflected in research projects.

REFERENCES

Benbow, S. M. and Jagus, C. E. (2002) Sexuality in older women with mental health problems. *Sexual and Relationship Therapy* 17(3): 261–270.

Bland, L. and Mort, F. (1997) Thinking sex historically, in L. Segal (ed.) *New Sexual Agendas*. London: Macmillan, pp. 17–31.

Brecher, E. M. (1984) *Love, Sex and Aging: A Consumers Union Report*. Boston: Little, Brown and Company.

Burr, V. (1995) *An Introduction to Social Constructionism*. London: Routledge.

Butler, J. (1990) *Gender Trouble: Feminism and the Subversion of Identity*. London: Routledge.

Coupland, J. (2000) Past the 'perfect kind of age'?: styling selves and relationships in over-50s dating advertisements. *Journal of Communication* 5(3): 9–30.

Deacon, S., Minichiello, V. and Plummer, D. (1995) Sexuality and older people: revisiting the assumptions. *Educational Gerontology* 21(5): 497–513.

Eve magazine: 'A week in the life of ... Liz Cowley, who is 74 this month'. April 2001, pp. 27–29.

Gergen, K. J. (1985) The social constructionist movement in modern psychology. *American Psychologist* 40: 266–275.

Greengross, W. and Greengross, S (1989) *Living, Loving and Ageing: Sexual Relationships in Later Life*. London: Age Concern England.

Jackson, S. and Scott, S. (eds) (1996) *Feminism and Sexuality: A Reader*. Edinburgh: Edinburgh University Press.

Johnson, A. M., Mercer, C. H., Copas, A. J., McManus, S., Wellings, K., Fenton, K. A., Korovessis, C., Macdowall, W., Nanchahal, K., Purdon, S. and Field, J. (2001) Sexual behaviour in Britain: partnerships, practices, and HIV risk behaviours. *The Lancet* 358(9296): 1835–1842.

Jones, R. L. (2002) 'That's very rude, I shouldn't be telling you that': older women talking about sex. *Narrative Inquiry* 12(1): 121–142.

Jones, R. L. (2003) *Older Women Talking About Sex: A Discursive Analysis*. Unpublished PhD thesis, The Open University, Milton Keynes.

Plummer, K. (1995) *Telling Sexual Stories: Power, Change and Social Worlds*. London: Routledge.

Rich, A. (1980) Compulsory heterosexuality and lesbian existence. *Signs* 5(4): 631–660.

Silverman, D. (1997) *Discourses of Counselling: HIV Counselling as Social Interaction*. London: Sage.

Starr, B. D. and Bakur, M. (1981) *The Starr-Weiner Report on Sex and Sexuality in the Mature Years*. London: W. H. Allen.

Verwoedt, A., Pfeiffer, E. and Wang, H. S. (1969) Sexual behavior in senescence, ii: patterns of sexual activity and interest. *Geriatrics* 24(2): 137–154.

Weg, R. B. (1983) *Sexuality in the Later Years: Roles and Behaviour*. London: Academic Press.

Wellings, K., Field, J., Johnson, A. M. and Wadsworth, J. (1994) *Sexual Behaviour in Britain: The National Survey of Sexual Attitudes and Lifestyles*. London: Penguin.

5

FINDING PEOPLE TO INTERVIEW
A study of the impact of family change on older people

SHEILA PEACE, JOANNA BORNAT, DAVID JONES AND BRIAN DIMMOCK

INTRODUCTION

Concern about the changing nature of family life assaults us daily. We are presently bombarded with information – from official surveys, research studies, media anecdote – about the experience of divorce, single mothers, absent fathers, the meaning of fatherhood, the lives of working women, the path towards gay marriage. The study reported here focused on a related area of interest; the impact upon the lives of older people of family break-up through divorce, separation, and remarriage and reconstitution. This has been a neglected area within the research on stepfamilies. We know something of the lives of those involved in these kinds of events and in particular about the impact of such family change on children (Burgoyne and Clark 1984; Wallerstein and Kelly 1980; Ferri 1984; Batchelor et al. 1994). But with some notable exceptions (see Thompson et al. 1990; Grundy 1995; Finch 1995; Jerrome 1996) relatively little has been discovered about their impact on older people within the UK. A more well developed literature exists within the USA (see Johnson 1988; Bengston et al. 1995). Yet, within an ageing population, concerns about family change in relation to a range of issues are of particular concern and importance, not only for individuals and their families, but also the wider society. These include caring arrangements; family transfers and inheritance; and grand parenting. A further, related concern, lies at the level of the meaning of family change for different generations and how life history effects our construction of meaning about the family.

This project was one of seventeen funded by the ESRC within its programme on 'Household and Population Change' (1994–1999), which had the broad aim of stimulating research on 'the interrelationship between household living arrangements and broader demographic change in the United Kingdom' (McRae 1999). Other projects within the programme were concerned with some of the areas outlined above, and they varied widely in terms of their approach: at one end involving secondary analysis of large data sets; at the other small scale qualitative studies. The *Impact of Family Change on Older People* project fell into the latter group of studies, and the purpose of this chapter is to discuss how we went about finding people with experience of family breakdown and reconstitution who would be willing to undertake an in-depth life history interview. The study was conducted over two years, with resources to employ one full-time research fellow and enable three academics a notional third of a day a week (Bornat et al. 1999).

OUR ORIGINAL AIMS

We had decided on a small-scale, in-depth qualitative approach and to locate the study in one place. We chose Luton, partly from convenience, but more importantly because it is a fairly average sized town – 171,671 at the then latest census (1991) – with a diverse multi-cultural population. Its industrial base had witnessed economic change within both long and newly established industries (car industry, millinery, light engineering). Of secondary importance was the fact that Luton had also been subject to considerable sociological study, being home to the famous 'Affluent Worker' study (Goldthorpe et al. 1969) and consequent follow-up work (Devine 1992). This historical and contextual information enabled us to embed our findings within a broader picture of a town that had also seen immense change over time particularly in employment patterns; changes which were reflected within our interviews.

So, having settled on a place, we needed to consider the people. Our unit of analysis was to be the individual, and our aim was for depth rather than breadth. The sample, therefore, was to be *purposeful* (non-probability) but we also sought to avoid *systematic bias*.

> The logic of purposeful sampling in qualitative methods is quite different from the logic of probabilistic sampling in statistics. The power of statistical sampling depends on selecting a truly random and representative sample which will permit confident generalisation from the sample to a larger population. The power of purposeful sampling lies in selecting information-rich cases for study in depth.
>
> (Patton 1987, pp. 51–52)

As Patton outlines here, we were looking for 'information-richness'; our primary concern was not with making generalisations. Given the uncharted nature of our area of interest, our purpose from the outset was always exploratory (see Arber 1993). We knew from reading the experiences of researchers such as Burgoyne and Clark in their study of stepfamilies (1978) that identifying our sample might prove problematic –

indeed they commented on their own methods of arriving at a sample of 40 stepfamilies as 'eclectic in the extreme' (1984, p. 32). But perhaps we thought at the outset that we would not have their problems. After all people were more aware of research into family life and these were now everyday subjects, weren't they?

Our approach to finding a sample was structured, and in this sense we did not equate 'purposeful' with 'convenient'. We began with a set of parameters that we felt needed to be met in order to fulfil our aims. These were based around issues of:

- ordinariness
- older sample
- intergenerational focus
- diversity
- opportunity/scheduling

First, we wanted to hear the experience of 'ordinary lives' from people who had experienced some form of family change. They were not necessarily people who saw themselves as belonging to a stepfamily. This meant that we decided not to obtain our sample through organisations such as 'STEPFAMILY' (a voluntary organisation that aims to provide mutual support and provide information for people who self-define as members of stepfamilies – see Batchelor et al. 1994 for research undertaken through this organisation). We also sought to avoid people who might have a particular point of view or reason for wishing to take part through being a member of an organisation or as a user of a service. Because of a concern over *systematic bias* we also decided not to advertise for volunteers.

Second, we were concerned to hear the views of older people and therefore set out to try to obtain a greater sample of people over retirement age. A third point, which is linked to this focus, was our interest in hearing the views of people from more than one generation with the same family. Our aim was to achieve this by gaining access to one person who would then put us in touch with another through a snow-balling effect.

Fourth, given the diverse cultural composition of the population in Luton we thought that we would reach a sub-sample of people from within the Asian community without targeting them in particular. Thus they would form part of the overall diverse picture that would incorporate a cultural dimension. Finally, from the outset we felt that a target population of approximately 80 interviews could be achieved within the time allotted to field work and that this would yield a manageable data set with sufficient depth. At an early stage we had estimated that by obtaining access to 30 family members who might suggest other family members to be interviewed we could arrive at a sample of 90–120 individuals. This estimate turned out to be over ambitious.

'SEEK AND YE SHALL FIND'

(a) Area sampling

We decided to target certain areas in Luton through a process of area sampling utilising the 1991 census data. Our criteria for choosing areas within the city were based on a desire for areas which, whilst having a higher than average older population, also differed in terms of social class and housing tenure: i.e. we wished to stress the differences between rather than within areas. Therefore we considered census data concerning:

- percentage of people over retirement age
- housing tenure – owner-occupation and local authority and private renting
- percentage unemployed

Using these criteria we chose three wards – identified on figure 5.1. They were:

Hightown – just to the north of the railway station. One of the oldest parts of the town with mixed light industry, including many original hatters firms, and predominantly terraced housing. Essentially a working class area with some more affluent areas surrounding park land. A mixed population of White, Asian and Afro-Caribbean families. Also a student population.

Icknield – to the north of Hightown. Predominantly a more middle-class residential area with a variety of semi-detached and detached housing built in the inter-war and post-war periods. Noted for park land within and adjacent to the area.

Farley Hill – built during the post-war expansion of Luton, this is a large local authority housing estate comprising blocks of low rise flats, bungalows and semi-detached houses. The estate has a secondary school and two primary schools, a community centre, churches, shops, pub, and sheltered housing for older people.

Figure 5.1 Luton

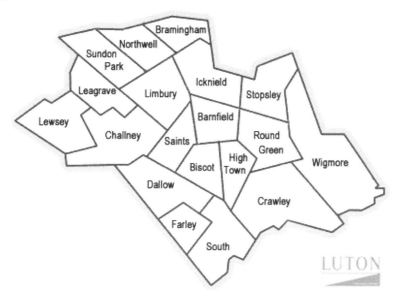

Some basic information concerning the characteristics of each of these wards is given in table 5.1. Consideration was also given at this point to the distribution of people from minority ethnic groups within the town. However, it soon became obvious that due to differences in the age structure of the populations from different ethnic groupings, our focus on older populations was to lead us away from the concentrations of Afro-Caribbeans, and to some extent Asian groups in the town. We decided at this point that age rather than ethnicity was our major concern.

Once we had chosen the three areas we decided to try and locate people primarily through (i) screening households within Enumeration Districts in each area, but subsequently, (ii) by contacting groups concerned with older people within in each area.

(b) Screening households

Each ward comprised at least 10 Enumeration Districts (EDs), i.e. approximately 200 households, and we decided that if we were interested in the experiences of 'ordinary' people we would need to screen every household. We began by identifying one predominantly residential ED from each ward, again chosen to be representative of the criteria outlined above, and obtained names and addresses from the Electoral Register.

Within this population base we then had to devise a screening instrument. We decided that as we were going to approach every household, we should devise an instrument which was multi-purpose:

- it introduced people to the study and gave a contact;
- it asked people two short attitudinal questions about their own attitudes towards marriage, and also encouraged them to write further about their views on 'the increasing rate of divorce, remarriage and stepfamilies';
- it asked a series of questions about their own characteristics and family experiences of divorce, separation and remarriage;
- it defined whom we were looking for at the interview stage of the project and asked people to let us know about their family circumstances.

All screening instruments were addressed to a named person and were accompanied by a pre-paid envelope for return. At an early stage, a pilot instrument was tested which asked people to tick a box if they did, or did not, wish to take part in the interview stage. As this appeared to give people a way of opting out of the study, rather than in to it, this was later abandoned.

PREPARATION FOR SCREENING

Door-to-door screening can place the researcher in a potentially vulnerable position, and at the same time may make the householder nervous. Therefore, we tried to make the process a more public one. The researcher always carried some form of identification from the University and we informed the local police of the dates and times we would be in the area and what we were doing. We also attempted to raise the profile of the project within the town by doing an interview on Three Counties Radio just before the screening period commenced, and also a report for the local press that was carried in two Luton papers.

Table 5.1 Characteristics of the three locations, 1991 Census

	Hightown	Icknield	Farley Hill		Hightown Ward	Icknield Ward	Farley Hill Ward
					%	%	%
Total population 1991	8,957	10,989	9,414	Age-groups			
White	85.00 %	93.20 %	87.90 %	0-14	17	18	21
Black (i)	4.10 %	2.30 %	4.20 %	15-19	5	7	6
I/P/B (ii)	8.20 %	5.00 %	6.70 %	20-29	24	14	17
				30-44	21	20	20
LA housing	11.80 %	8.90 %	38.70 %	45-59	13	20	14
Owner-occupied	69.10 %	86.20 %	53.90 %	60-69	7	10	12
Unemployed	11.80 %	6.20 %	14.10 %	70-79	7	6	8
Population 75 years and over	8.00 %	6.00 %	5.00 %	80+	5	3	3
				N =	8,957	10,989	9,414
				Sex			
(i) Black Caribbean, Black African and Black Other combined	(ii) Indian, Pakistani and Bangladeshi combined			male	50	49	49
				female	50	51	51

SCREENING COMMENCES

Within the first three EDs, we undertook an experiment by posting the documents to people in Hightown and delivering door to door in Icknield and Farley Hill. In addition, the researcher who delivered in Icknield and Farley Hill also returned at an agreed time and date to collect screening instruments from certain streets. We embarked on these various options in order to see whether our response rate might be improved by the different methods. After two months we reassessed our position. While the pick-up method produced a higher rate of returns, it did not yield any more contacts for interviews than the postal method. For example, within one street in Icknield, we sent 50 screening questionnaires and picked up 17 (57 per cent) but yielded no interviews compared to a street in Hightown where we sent 50 screening questionnaires, received 6 (12 per cent) by post and achieved one interview. As the in-depth interviews were to form our main data set we decided to send out more questionnaires and rely on a postal response.

(c) Contacting groups

Whilst our screening programme was underway, we felt that it was important to talk with groups of older people within the chosen area of study. We wanted to learn more about how people perceived the issues surrounding family change and the language they used to speak about the issues. Therefore, we contacted local groups for older people within the three areas, and our request to tell people about the study usually led to us being invited as guest speakers at group meetings. Thus we covered groups such as: the Retired Civil Servants Association; the Greenhills Day Centre; the Co-operative Women's Guild and other church groups.

We also made use of contacts within Luton University, putting an advertisement about the project into the University's staff magazine and gaining access through the Social Work Department to the local social services managers in each of our three areas. Meeting with the local academic and social services groups was important in terms of alerting health and social welfare professionals to our work and hearing directly their views on how family change affected the lives of older people. These discussions made us aware of the special schemes and services for older people and, whilst we were not keen to identify people as service users, we did follow up some specific scheme such as a day centre for Asian Elders.

We had not intended using these contacts as a main source of our sample, but in the outcome they supplemented the screening exercise.

ARRIVING AT A SAMPLE

In total we sent out 1796 screening questionnaires during a ten-month period. From this number we had 249 returned completed, and these completed questionnaires form an interesting data set in their own right.

The characteristics of this group are given in table 5.2, and this can be compared with the basic information on the three wards given earlier and data on age and marital status for Luton as a whole given in table 5.3. In comparing our respondents in each area with the ward profiles, we could see that in Icknield and Farley Hill the respondents were much older than the general populations, particularly within the 60 to 80 year age bands. Hightown respondents were much more in line with the ward profile, although we picked up slightly more people in the 34–44 age band. The sex ratios also showed that a greater number of women responded to the screening questionnaires, particularly in Icknield and Farley Hill.

Data from Luton as a whole [table 5.3.] showed the preponderance of divorced people within the middle years population – with more women divorced across a wider age-span. It was difficult to compare this data with our respondents from the screening questionnaire because we had employed a wider range of categories for marriage breakdown. The higher percentage of older people in our sample greatly increased the number of widowed respondents compared with the total population of Luton, and this was particularly the case for older women. The percentage of those divorced was not particularly high amongst our respondents; yet they were higher than those in the overall Luton population, where 4 per cent of men and 5 per cent of women were recorded as divorced in the 1991 census. The figures for Hightown indicated the greater number of younger single people who responded in that area.

The information from this data set enabled us to identify 120 people who could be potential interviewees based on (a) the closeness of the relationship in terms of distance between individual and family member experiencing break; i.e. who had experienced family breakdown themselves, or were the parent, child or sibling of someone who had experienced a family breakdown; and (b) the closeness of the relationship in terms of emotional involvement.

Table 5.2 Characteristics of respondents to the screening questionnaire

	H	I	FH		H	I	FH
Age groups	%	%	%	**Marital status**			
15-20				Married	28	50	32
21-30	16	11	11	Live with partner	10	3	6
31-45	33	12	19	Separated	5	4	2
46-60	22	23	23	Divorced	9	7	12
61-70	10	22	20	Widowed	19	25	31
71-80	9	26	23	Single	22	9	17
81 plus	9	5	5	Remarried	6	2	
Mis. cases		1		Mis. cases		1	
	N= 67	N= 117	N= 65		N = 67	N = 117	N = 65
Sex							
M	43	32	37				
F	58	68	63				

Self separated, divorced or remarried	%	%	%	**Member of family separated, divorced or remarried**			
Yes	32	22	22	Yes	77	75	63
No	21	26	14	No	51	48	72
	N= 67	N= 117	N= 65		N = 67	N = 117	N = 65

Key: H = Hightown I = Icknield FH = Farley Hill

Table 5.3 Characteristics of Luton, 1991 Census

LUTON %	Men marital status				
Age-groups	*single*	*married*	*widowed*	*divorced*	*total population*
15-19	99	1	<111111	<1	5,648
20-29	68	31	0.1	2	15,918
30-44	20	72	0.3	8	18,431
45-59	9	80	1.5	9.5	13,545
60-69	9	77	7	6	6,759
70-79	8	71	17	3	3,788
80+	4	56	39	1	1,368
Total population by marital status	49	44	2	4	
%	Women marital status				
Age-groups	*single*	*married*	*widowed*	*divorced*	*total population*
15-19	97	2.99		0.01	5,450
20-29	53	44	0.1	2.9	16,608
30-44	12	76	1	11	17,559
45-59	4	78	7	11	12,909
60-69	5	65	24	6	6,576
70-79	6	42	49	3	5,101
80+	8	18	73	1	3,129
Total population by marital status	42	44	9	5	

Following an initial attempt at writing to people with pre-arranged times for an interview, we found that we had to introduce yet another stage into the process, writing to all 120 people to ask if they would like to be interviewed and getting them to suggest suitable times. Forty-nine interviews were obtained directly through this process. The remainder were obtained through the alternative approach of group contact, bringing the total number of interviews completed to 60. Because some of these involved more than one person, they included 71 people.

COMPARING THE FINAL SAMPLE WITH OUR ORIGINAL AIMS

Whilst at times it felt as though we would never 'find someone to talk to' we had arrived at a sample of 60 interviews with 71 people, which was not too far outside our original target of 80 people. The personal experience of marriage breakdown for the interviewees is given in table 5.4, which shows that we did achieve our aim of over-sampling amongst the older age groups whilst maintaining a spread across the generations. At this stage it proved very difficult to embed the final sample within the data at ward level or at the level of respondents to our screening questionnaire. The range of personal or family experience however was in line with the wider response.

However, we were less successful in meeting some of our initial aims. We found it well nigh impossible to get people to refer us on to other members of their family who would be able to give a different perspective on the same family story. In the main, people acted a 'gatekeepers' to other family members. It appeared that they felt vulnerable and a little wary of other family members' opinions of what they were doing. Indeed, it could be that the more intimate people became in terms of the personal details they divulged during in-depth interviewing, the less likely people were to allow access to other kin. However, this is not to say that we had to completely abandon our ideas of making comparisons between generations. Our comparisons could not be made around the same story within one family; but we could explore common issues across age-groups.

We also found that we did not pick up as many people from minority ethnic groups as we had hoped. In the end, there were only three Asian respondents within the sample. We realised fairly early on in the screening process that we would have to target groups directly if we wished to include a substantial number of people from minority ethnic groups, and as the project was exploratory in nature, it was decided that

Table 5.4 The final purposive sample
60 interviews. 71 individuals   28 men and 43 women

| | Men | | | |
	divorced	*widowed*	*remarried*	*total*
Older	1	3	3	16
Middle	7	0	6	10
Younger	0	0	-	2

| | Women | | | |
	divorced	*widowed*	*remarried*	*total*
Older	4	6	3	14
Middle	16	0	13	24
Younger	3	0	1	5

this would not be possible given our schedule and the elaborate process
we had been through in order to reach a modest sample.

DISCUSSION – WHAT WE LEARNED

This was a two-year study and the first year was dominated by finding
people to talk to. Our experiences here show that you should not
underestimate the time needed for sampling in potentially sensitive areas.
We had thought at the outset that given the current, very public debate
about the future of family life, people would be open to being interviewed
about their own family change; but this did not prove to be the case.
Many of the screening instruments, which might have yielded a potential
interview, were returned to us with the comment 'please do not contact
further'. Certainly, it proved impossible to carry out our proposed
snowballing method amongst those who were eventually interviewed. The
consequence of this was that in our study of older people within families
that have experienced breakdown and change, we had to rely for an
intergenerational focus on the views of unrelated people from different
age groups. This meant that we had to change the focus of interviewing
and that consequently affected our analysis.

Of particular interest is the fact that we deliberately did not use the
term 'stepfamily' within our hunt for interviewees. If we had used this
term, we feel sure that we would have obtained a very different sample.
We were seeking the views of 'ordinary' people whose families had
experienced some form of breakdown and reconstitution. As we have
seen, between a quarter and a third of the respondents to our screening

instrument had direct personal experience of marriage breakdown, and between two-thirds and three-quarters had family members with such experience. These figures are indicative of the fact that such changes are 'common' experiences and this is what we sought to capture.

Finally, the structured nature of our purposive sampling was a deliberate attempt to avoid systemic bias within our sample. While we were not concerned with representativeness, we were concerned that the sample reflected the lives of 'ordinary' people. Of course, ultimately, our sample did self-select, in that they chose to be interviewed. But we did feel that by being able to embed this group of interviews within the knowledge gained through the screening questionnaires and our understanding of life within Luton more widely, we were able to contain systematic bias within the study.

REFERENCES

Arber, S. (1993) Designing samples, in N. Gilbert (ed.) *Researching Social Life*. London: Sage Publications.

Batchelor, J., Dimmock, D. and Smith, D. (1994) *Stepfamilies Understanding*: *What can be Learned from Callers to the Stepfamily Telephone Counselling Service*. London: Stepfamily.

Bengston, V. L., Warner Schaie, K. and Burton, L. M. (eds) (1995) *Adult Intergenerational Relations: Effects of Social Change*. New York: Springer.

Bornat, J., Dimmock, B., Jones, D. and Peace, S. (1999) The impact of family change on older people: the case of stepfamilies, in S. McRae (ed.) *Changing Britain: Families and Households in the 1990s*. Oxford: Oxford University Press, pp. 248–262.

Burgoyne, J. and Clarke, D. (1984) *Making a Go of It: A Study of Stepfamilies in Sheffield*. London: Routledge and Kegan Paul.

Devine, F. (1992) *Affluent Workers Revisited*. Edinburgh: Edinburgh University Press.

Ferri, E. (1984) *Stepchildren*: *A National Study*. Windsor: NFER Nelson Publishing.

Finch, J. (1995) Obligation and commitment, in I. Allen and E. Perkins (eds) *The Future of Family Care For Older People*. London: HMSO.

Goldthorpe, J. (1969) *The Affluent Worker*. London: Routledge and Kegan Paul.

Grundy, E. (1995) Demographic influences on the future of family care, in I. Allen, and E. Perkins (eds) *The Future of Family Care For Older People*. London: HMSO.

Jerrome, D. (1996) Continuity and change in the study of family relationships, *Ageing and* Society 16(1): 93–104.

Johnson, C. L. (1988) *Ex Familia: Grandparents, Parents and Children Adjust to Divorce*. New Brunswick: Rutgers University Press.

McRae, S. (ed.) (1999) *Changing Britain: Families and Households in the 1990s*. Oxford: Oxford University Press.

Patton, M. J. 101987) *How to Use Qualitative Methods in Evaluation*. London: Sage Publications.

Thompson, P., Itkin, K. and Abendstrom, C. (1990) *I Don't Feel Old: The Experience of Later Life*. Oxford: Oxford University Press.

Wallerstein, J. and Kelly, J. (1980) *Surviving the Break-up: How Children and Parents Cope with Divorce*. New York: Basic Books.

6

SOCIAL INTERACTIONS IN URBAN PUBLIC PLACES
Participative method and recruitment strategies

ANDREW CLARK, CAROLINE HOLLAND, SHEILA PEACE AND JEANNE KATZ

Public places are important to people of all ages. The government has committed itself to providing quality public places as part of its goal to improve the quality of our towns and cities and many studies have shown that access to public places is important to health. Studies have also shown that good public places can benefit local economies, encourage people to spend more time in shops and businesses, and raise house prices. But more than this, public places are important because almost everybody uses them. Whether this involves attending a meeting at a community centre, walking the dog in a local park, taking children to a nearby playground, shopping in a busy shopping centre or just meeting friends by a well-known local landmark, public places are part of our everyday lives. They are places where teenagers can hang out, children play, and adults meet friends: places surely that allow 'community' to exist and flourish.

Yet in spite of the rhetoric of policy and the commonplaces of received knowledge about them, we actually know very little about how we use public places, and why they are important to us. Do different groups of people use places differently? How do people of different ages relate to each other in these places? What affect does the time of day or even the weather have on what people do in them? Does the presence of particular groups of people create problems for others? Does design influence behaviour in any way?

These are some of the questions that we have been considering in research funded by the Joseph Rowntree Foundation under their 'Public Places' programme (on-going at the time of writing). The project 'Social Interactions in Urban Public Places' uses a multi-method approach to gathering data about what people actually make of public spaces. We decided:

- to concentrate on one 'typical' town. This needed to be easily accessible from Milton Keynes (our base) and we looked at towns within a 70 mile radius before settling on Aylesbury, the administrative centre of Buckinghamshire;

- to use a non-participant observation method so that we could get closer to finding out what people actually do in public places at different times of day and different parts of the year;
- to use a participative method that would allow local people to take part in the collection, analysis and dissemination of data. This would involve training people in non-participant observation, and supporting them in their work. Observers would be paid at a good hourly rate and we would recruit volunteers from across the age range, but with a particular emphasis on young (16–25) and older (50+) participants.

METHODS

Our aim is to produce comprehensive data and analysis on social interactions in key public places within Aylesbury, and to relate our findings to emerging local and national policy agendas on public space. To do this, the project encompasses the key central public spaces in Aylesbury, and two locations further away from the town centre, detailed in table 6.1.

To try to capture a year-round picture of what is happening in these places at different times of the day, we developed a combination of checklist/mapped recording (figure 6.1, p. 82), and field diaries (figure 6.2 p. 83). We are carrying out this part of the study with the help of trained local people. (Here they are sometimes termed 'observers' with relation to the observation work itself, but otherwise we prefer to call them co-researchers to acknowledge their involvement in the analysis and evolution of the project). Our ethnographic approach encourages the co-researchers to focus their observation on particular spaces (micro-sites) within each study location, and then on particular individuals, activities or groups of individuals within these micro-sites. This is to produce a more nuanced account of site-specific geographies of public space, revealing the strategies and locations of territorial practices by certain groups, as well as producing detailed observations on particular processes of interaction. The co-researchers work in pairs, with one person completing the checklist and map, while the other completes the field diary. All co-researchers are trained to use both techniques so that they can alternate as required. It was emphasised to co-researchers that they would be using a covert observational technique that would require them to avoid as far as possible any intervention in the situations they would observe (with clear exceptions related to safety and legal requirements).

Table 6.1 Aylesbury: key study locations

Location	Features
The Vale Park	Created in the 1930s and modelled on formal Victorian designs, the park is located less than five minutes walk from the centre of Aylesbury and is seen as 'the town park' rather than a local one
The Grand Union Canal - towpath	Runs close to the town centre yet remains a distinct, separate space. Due for extensive redevelopment as a leisure facility. Preliminary observations suggested a variety of users including walkers, canal-boat residents, anglers, street-drinkers and homeless people.
The Market Square	A cobbled open space with an 18th century courthouse, clock tower, and several statues; bounded by the two shopping malls (below). Open markets are held at least three days a week.
Hale Leys shopping centre	The older of two indoor shopping centres in Aylesbury centre. It is also used as a main thoroughfare between the High Street and the Market Square.
Friarsgate Shopping Centre	The newer of two indoor shopping centres in Aylesbury; larger and with more open internal space and seating.
Kingsbury Square	Directly adjacent to the Market Square. Its redevelopment under the 'sustainable communities' initiative was completed in late 2004, producing a cobbled and paved open space with a futuristic water feature.
The High Street	The original main shopping street, now partly pedestrianised, it connects the Market Square to the Vale Park.
Walton Court Shopping Precinct	Typical of many neighbourhood shopping precincts built to serve post-war housing estates. Ground floor shops face inwards to an enclosed courtyard, with offices and residential accommodation on the floor above.

Fairford Leys Village Centre	A large, private development on the periphery of town. It appears to have been designed under the ethos of 'new urbanism' (compact, esoteric buildings designed around a neo-traditional centre reminiscent of village or 'community' centres in the past.

We asked them to try to be as 'invisible' as possible and not interrupt the activities and behaviours of individuals in the places they were investigating. However we would not be secretive about the research and if they were approached about what they were doing, we asked them to provide the enquirer with a handout about the project.

RECRUITING CO-RESEARCHERS

We wanted to observe the selected sites at different times of the day from early morning until late at night and in all kinds of weather. The observation timeframe is October 2004 to September 2005. This required many hours of observation and we needed to recruit people who would be able to work unusual hours on a very part-time basis. We expected that we would need to recruit more people as the project continued and some observers dropped out of the project. However, recruiting people as co-researchers was not completely straightforward, partly because of the project design's fairly unusual requirements:

- The research needed to be kept low key. While the observations were not to be covert or secretive, we did not want widespread publicity about the project because we wanted to minimise general awareness of the presence of observers – both for their protection and to reduce the possibility of 'observer effect'. Hence we decided on minimum publicity, restricted to a small number of handouts distributed to targeted groups – and no media attention, at least until the observations were completed.
- We required co-researchers from all age groups but particularly wanted to include younger (16 – 25) or older (50 +) age groups and we were particularly interested in inter-generational involvement in both method and interaction.
- We needed most of the co-researchers to be familiar with Aylesbury, but we also needed some people who were relatively unfamiliar with the study locations so that we could consider 'geographical bias'. This meant that we had to recruit both Aylesbury residents (and

workers/students) and people who did not live in Aylesbury but could conveniently get to it.

- We needed our co-researchers to be enthusiastic and open to challenges of a research process that was both unusual and likely to change over the course of the project.

The initial recruitment was conducted through a twofold framework:

i) We targeted social activities and places likely to be frequented by younger and older people, namely:
- The Youth Connexions Centre (Here one of the youth workers helped to identify people who might match our requirements as co-researchers.)
- A youth theatre and arts centre
- The University of the Third Age
- Age Concern Buckinghamshire (Here a senior officer also helped with suggestions.)

Both the Connexions and Age Concern representatives joined our advisory group, which also includes other local stakeholders and interested academics.

We also approached some of the local secondary schools, but they declined to pass the information about the project on to students. While there are arguments to be made about the role of gatekeepers in recruiting and sampling people for social research, in this case we were purposively looking for individuals who would be able to carry out the research rather than a random sample or other bias-free group of research 'subjects'. The recommendation of the gatekeepers, who had been told about the project in detail, also lent a degree of familiarity and hence trustworthiness to the research as it was proposed to potential co-researchers.

ii) Snowballing. We explained to potential recruits that they would be working in pairs or occasionally in teams. As we trained them, we invited co-researchers to introduce other people and this proved a good way of increasing our recruitment and producing some good working partnerships. It has also produced to date two mother-daughter teams.

Five months into the project we had recruited and trained 31 people, including 17 people aged under 24 and 10 aged over 50. Fortunately we have experienced an excellent level of interest and enthusiasm from the co-researchers. Most had been attracted to the project because of the rate of pay as much as because they saw the project as different and interesting. But it became clear to those who worked over winter and experienced great discomfort at times, and quite a lot of boredom on some days, that the apparently high payment rate was far from excessive.

What has kept people with the project, apart from the pay, has been the negotiability of working hours and their intrinsic interest in the study. We have tried to encourage this by involving them in our thinking about the direction and analysis of the project. Co-researchers who had been working for several months were invited to de-briefing and analysis sessions at the end of the winter season where we were able to discuss some of the policy and academic issues about public space and talk through their own experiences of observing in our study locations. The co-researchers made suggestions ranging from categories for analysis of the data to ways of extending the scope of the study in future work. They are fully aware that in addition to the intergenerational focus of the observations, we also want to look at whether there is any difference in the data produced by older and younger co-researchers and in their experiences of being involved in this kind of work – and they tend to see this as another interesting aspect of the project.

REFLECTIONS ON RECRUITMENT

As we had expected, recruitment to this project is an ongoing process. We had hoped that some people would be able to stay with the project throughout the observation phase, but we knew that others would only want or be able to work with us for shorter periods of time, and this has been the case. Despite the winter conditions however, all the older co-researchers who started doing observations in November or December are, to date, still involved. In reflecting on the recruitment methods we adopted and the people we recruited as a result, we have found:

- An initial shortage of observers aged over 70, and older men in general, and a lack of observers with motor disabilities. The pragmatics of outdoor work in winter may have influenced this; and snowballing in particular may have by-passed older men. We aim to address these issues as we recruit more people, and because we have kept the recruitment low-key, there are other organisations such as interest groups for older men, that we have not yet targeted. However, we may be experiencing a gender/age difference.

- Bias – friends recruiting friends etc. It could be argued to have resulted in a rather homogenous group of co-researchers observing in uncritical pairs. Yet within the group as a whole we have differences in ages, experience, and relationships with the study locations; and as people often observe with people other than their friends we have not found in practice that this has been a problem.
- Emphasis placed on payment – how would the project have been different without the benefit of good funding for the participative method?
- As in life, not all observers get on well with each other and we have had to deal with this. However these occasional frictions have certainly not been the result of age differences.
- Issues of some co-researchers wanting to work more than we could afford them to, given our intention to spread the observations among the co-researchers. We have needed to balance co-researcher enthusiasm with the systems to support the aims of the project.
- Problems of recruiting observers during the evenings. Only eight of the observers have been willing to do observations after 6.00pm during the winter months. Most of the observers also prefer to avoid very early starts, and a few do not want to work at weekends. In general we have tried to accommodate observers' preferences within the timetable of required observations, with the Research Fellow and the rest of the team covering some of the more unsociable hours. We expect this to be less of a problem in the lighter evenings but we are also looking more 'evening' observers.

WORKING WITH 'PARTICIPANTS' AS 'CO-RESEARCHERS'

So far, the enthusiasm of the co-researchers has worked very much in our favour and kept people engaged even during the worst of the winter weather. But knowing that we need to maintain this enthusiasm and avoid 'observer burn-out', we scheduled breaks in the observations and ran a first round of analysis sessions with co-researchers. We have tried to keep our co-researchers fully informed about the project both in training and as it has progressed, including discussions about our rationales for any changes to the method (such as altering micro-locations, or changing observation times).

However our co-researchers necessarily 'missed out' on the initial stages of the research (question development and project design). While they can have input to the analysis and direction of the project, they cannot determine how the project proceeds. They have a participatory role, but it was defined for them before they began. All of this begs the questions, whose research? Whose results? In the end the professional academic team must take responsibility for the project and how the data are interpreted and presented. Researchers need to think hard about what 'participation' means in practice. To what extend can participants be involved in research that they did not conceive or design, and for which they are not ultimately responsible? What is in it for them other than financial payment? The boundaries of rights and responsibilities need to be clear.

One of the benefits of a participatory approach can be a more transparent research process and perhaps a democratisation of the use of 'public' funding. However this can expose the research and the researchers to criticism, especially if things do not go strictly to plan. We have found that we do need to be able to give a good account of the research and our reasons for doing it. The interpretive, exploratory and participative aspects of the method we chose to use are often questioned by potential observers and others. Researchers using participative methods need to be able to deal with public scrutiny – and to establish academic support for themselves.

We have found that there is a much greater than usual need for strong administrative and management support when doing research of this kind. In addition to the academic content the project involves a lot of management. Simply setting up systems for data retrieval, co-researcher payments and timetabling was very time-consuming and potential funders of this kind of research need to be aware that participative projects need time, money and structured support. Equally, academic institutions need an unaccustomed 'small-business-like' flexibility to deal properly with the day-to-day administration of this kind of project.

As the academics responsible for the quality of the data produced by the co-researchers, we found that there were questions in our own minds about what we would be able to produce using this method. Would the co-researchers be able to do what we asked them? Would they do it well? Inevitably the quality of data has been mixed, and we continue to advise co-researchers where necessary, but many are able to produce interesting and detailed accounts of what they have seen.

The co-researchers started out as paid volunteers, interested in the project but typically with no experience of research. By now many of them are becoming experts both in observation and in the daily life of Aylesbury. They now have more practical knowledge than anyone else about how people use the public places that they have been observing for months. For some of them this is producing tensions, as yet not fully resolved, in their status. Are they still essentially goodwill-volunteers, or are they paid contractors, or semi-professional researchers? Some of the co-researchers are very keen for a deeper involvement with the project, e.g. with the analysis and dissemination, and more so than we anticipated at the outset. While this is welcome, it could produce tensions about who 'owns' the final analysis and we will need to find a way to deal with the viewpoints of everyone that has been involved.

Some of the most engaged and consistent co-researchers have been among the group aged over 50. However to date we have recruited much fewer people in this age group than people aged under 25 (see table 6.2).

Table 6.2 Profile of observers recruited in the first six months

	Male	Female	Total
Under 24	7	10	17
25-49	1	3	4
Over 50	1	9	10
Total	9	22	31

There are several reasons why the work may initially have been less interesting to people in this age group than to the younger people - who are predominantly students or taking a 'gap-year'. Firstly, we started the fieldwork in the winter season with a likelihood of cold or rainy weather conditions and early nights. Second, for some potential participants there were tax/benefits implications of payment for the work. Third, the younger people were especially active in introducing other potential recruits, and some of the older ones also introduced younger people.

One of the most interesting features of this research is that it includes older people rather than concentrating on them. They are part of the profile of co-researchers; and their activities are represented in the intergenerational focus of the observation data. They are part of the context both of the research and of the emerging patterns of public life in Aylesbury. In addition to the mother/daughter pairs, many of the older co-researchers have now worked with younger observers as well as with their usual partners and we hope that the experiences of similar-age and intergenerational co-working will produce some interesting analysis.

Both the older and younger co-researchers include people who have come into contact with research before, for example professionally or in courses, and people who have not. There has been some discussion about what constitutes 'science' and 'evidence', and in general co-researchers of all ages are open to thinking about what they are doing and why they are doing it. All the co-researchers have their own positionalities, pre-existing ideas, etc., especially where social research is concerned. We do not regard these as challenges or barriers to be worked through/overcome (i.e. as 'bias'), but rather as benefits to the research in reflecting the myriad 'ways of seeing' the world that are being brought to bear on how people interpret their environments.

However we have had to think about how strenuous the research can be. The research team also carried out observations during the winter months and we found that two hours was about the most that could be done at a time without a break and this is the preference of most of the older co-researchers. We expect that this need to pace the observations will also apply if there is a hot summer. The intention is to balance the co-researchers' general preference for blocks of observation time with the need not to over-stretch them, whatever their age, and to protect the quality of the data.

At this stage in the research we are expecting to recruit and train more co-researchers as some of the younger observers leave the project (e.g. for University, travel, or full-time employment). We will be actively looking for more older co-researchers and especially for more older men to help complement our observations of Aylesbury with reflections on the gender and age differences, if any, in the way that co-researchers have seen and recorded the social interactions before them. What we do believe already is that involving the co-researchers in this study has been hard work, time consuming and costly; but without doubt crucial to the generation of the data we are seeking, and very rewarding and revealing both for them and for us.

Checklist for observations
Only include those USING rather than passing through the site.

Observer 17   Time 11·35   Date 15·10   Weather Bit brighter now!.

Person	Ethnicity	Sex M/F	Age Baby	Child	Young teen	Older teen	Adult	Older adult	Group size	Brief comment on what they are doing
1	W	F						✔	1	Sitting on bench waiting with shopping
2	W	M					✔		1	Workman picking up litter.
3	W	m					✔		2	chatting by benches
4	W	B						✔	2	Stopped to get sweets out of bag
5	W	F						✔	1	sitting on bench
6	W	M					✔		1	using mobile
7	W	F	✔	✔			✔		5	ladies with pushchairs -chatting
8	W	F						✔	1	sitting on bench.
9	W	M					✔	✔	2	chatting
10	W	F						✔	1	putting shopping away in bag

TURN OVER IF NECESSARY

Figure 6.1 Sample checklist

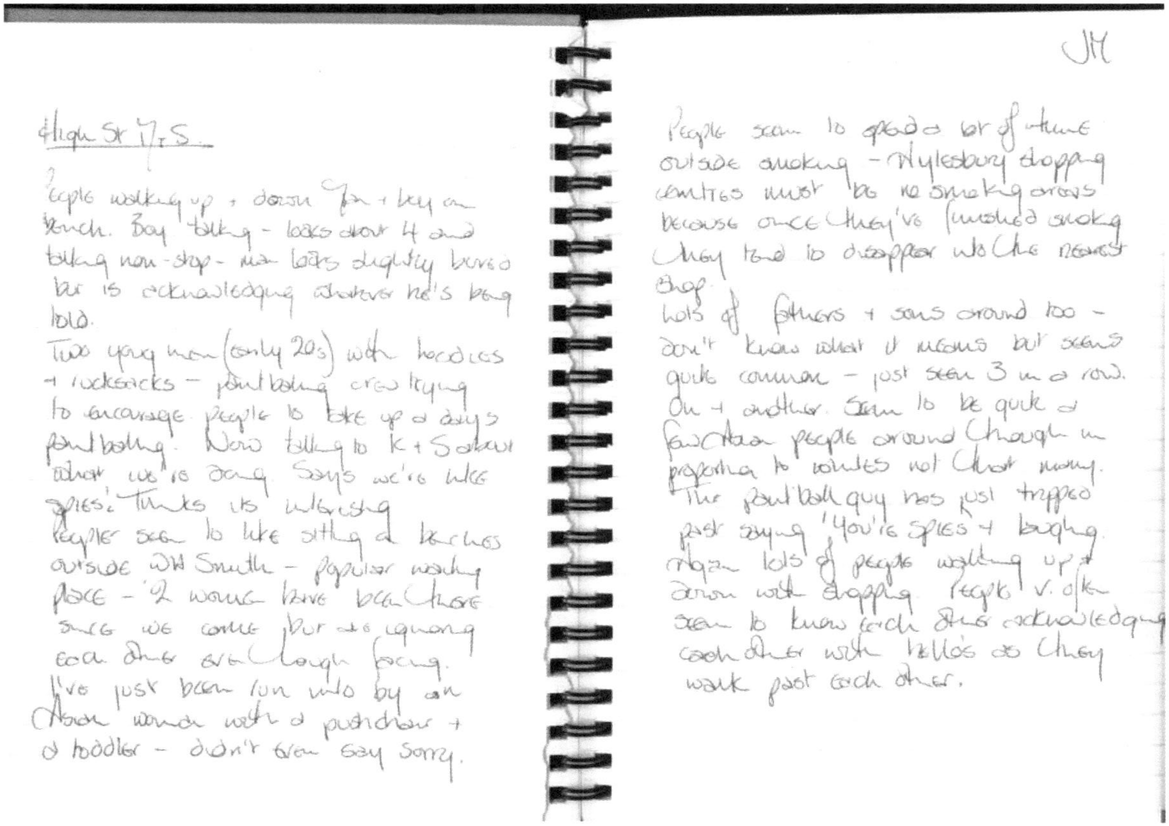

High St 17 S

People walking up + down for + buy a lunch. Boy talking - looks older than — tall'g man day- he looks slightly bored he is eavesdropping anyway he's reg told

Two young men (only 20's) with hoodies + rucksacks - (rucksacks) are trying to encourage people to take up a daily subscription. Keep talking to K + Sakur when we're doing. Says we're wide ... Thinks its weird. people seem to like sitting at benches outside JH Smith - popular meeting place - "I wanna have breakfast here we come for a quarry tea. She ate lunch here. I've just been for into by an older woman with a pushchair + a toddler - don't even say sorry.

People seem to speak a lot of — outside smoking - anylesburg shopping centres must be no smoking areas because once they've finished smoking they tend to disappear into the street.

Bag
Lots of others + sees around too - don't know what it means but seems quite common - just seen 3 in a row. Oh - another item to be quite a factor. people around through in general to adults not that many. The football guy has just tipped past saying "you're safe + begging .... lots of people walking up + down with shopping. People v. discr ...... to know each other's acknowledged each other with hellos as they walk past each other.

Figure 6.2 Sample field diary

The Authors

Members of CABS, the Faculty of Health and Social Care, the Open University:

Professor Joanna Bornat, Professor of Oral History

Dr Andrew Clark, Research Fellow

Dr Caroline Holland, Research Associate and Chair of CABS

Dr Jeanne Katz, Director of Post Graduate Studies

Dr Rebecca L. Jones, Lecturer (Health and Social Care)

Jane Montague, Research Student

Dr Sheila Peace, Senior Lecturer, Associate Dean/Director of Research

---

Brian Dimmock, Principal Lecturer, School of Health and Social Sciences, University of Gloucestershire

David Jones, Senior Lecturer, School of Social Sciences, Media and Cultural Studies, University of East London

Thomas Scharf, Director, Centre for Social Gerontology, School of Social Relations, Keele University